Wonder Writers

Teacher's Writing Resource 5

Wonder Writers®: **Teacher's Writing Resource — Grade 5**

Published in the United States by Rigby
a division of Reed Elsevier Inc.
1000 Hart Road
Barrington, IL 60010-2627
800-822-8661

© 2002 Rigby Education

WonderWriters® is a registered trademark of Reed Elsevier Inc.

07 06 05 04 03 02
10 9 8 7 6 5 4 3 2 1

Printed in Hong Kong

ISBN 0-7578-2060-3

Visit Rigby on the World Wide Web at http://www.rigby.com

Rigby

Table of Contents

Introduction

Writing, like reading, is a meaning-making process. As writers compose, they think about what they want to write, write their ideas, and speak their thoughts. They read their writing and revise it to shape their ideas and find their own voices as authors. Students engaged in authentic writing experiences within balanced literacy approaches learn how to write and how to be writers who naturally and comfortably use the writing process.

Wonder Writers was developed to support teachers as they teach writing and to encourage students to want to write. *Wonder Writers* for Grade 5 is comprised of this *Teacher's Writing Resource*—which includes 64 Writing Mini-lessons, teacher notes to accompany the 32 Writing Strategy Cards, and 32 Student Activity Pages—plus the *Writer's Handbook*. *Wonder Writers* provides lessons and writing activities that engage students as they learn the skills, strategies, and techniques of "real" writers.

The *Teacher's Writing Resource* carefully outlines the design, content, and process of the Writing Mini-lessons and Writing Strategy Cards and shows you how they can both be woven easily into the balanced literacy practices in your classroom.

- The developmentally appropriate Writing Mini-lessons are designed to let you model and teach the writing process as students are engaged as real writers.

- The Writing Strategy Cards and Student Activity Pages guide your classroom exploration of the strategies, techniques, and behaviors of writers.

- Students will make important reading and writing connections through these literacy experiences.

With *Wonder Writers,* you will grow as a more reflective and effective teacher of writing, while your students grow as writers.

puncation
Grammer
special word
useage
Spelling
caps,
proreading

About the Mini-lessons

By learning the procedures, techniques, and skills that writers use during the writing process, students learn to make decisions about their writing as "real authors." The *Wonder Writers* Mini-lessons are organized according to the steps of the writing process. As you can see in the chart below, these closely mirror the tasks and behaviors readers use before, during, and after reading.

Readers	Writers
Setting the Scene • activate and build prior knowledge • select topics and genre • determine purpose • consider audience of text	***Prewriting*** • activate and build prior knowledge • select topics and genre • determine purpose • consider audience
Reading the Text • practice skills/strategies to read words • use strategies to create meaning • monitor meaning • use sensory images • build a flow of meaning	***Drafting*** • practice skills/strategies to transcribe words • use strategies to create meaning • monitor meaning • express sensory images • create a flow of ideas
Returning to the Text • ask questions • revisit text to revise meaning • strive for accuracy • focus on features of text • reflect to personalize text	***Revising*** • ask questions • revisit writing to clearly convey meaning • strive for accuracy • return to writing to examine features • reflect to personalize writing
Responding to the Text • go beyond text to extend learning • share their responses • value the literature • express their voices • feel success • want to reread the literature	***Publishing*** • create writing that extends their thinking • share their writing • value their own compositions • establish their voices • feel success • want to reread their writing

Mini-lessons

Each of the 64 Mini-lessons has a clearly defined focus and a supportive teaching sequence. A suggested teaching sequence for the Mini-lessons helps you link reading and writing skills and strategies with those taught in the *Rigby Literacy Comprehension Quarterlies.* You may choose to present two lessons weekly or select specific lessons as needed to meet the needs of the writers in your classroom. The Mini-lessons may be presented in small groups or with the whole class.

Step of the Writing Process
The Mini-lessons are organized in five sections that follow the steps of the writing process. See pages 10 and 11 for further explanation.

Drafting

Writing an Essay: Identifying Facts and Opinions

Lesson Background
Discusses the writing development of Grade 5 students and explains the purpose of the lesson.

You Will Need

- transparency markers
- overhead projector
- overhead transparencies of BLM 34 and BLM 34A ("The Case for Sneakers" and "America's Favorite Shoe")
- a collection of books that have opinions expressed by several contributors such as ones compiled by Michelle Roehm

Lesson Background

Students are constantly sharing opinions on many subjects. They also express their views in writing. This mini-lesson helps students understand the difference between fact and opinion and the need to support their viewpoints with factual details.

Teaching the Lesson

1. Display "The Case for Sneakers" on the overhead projector and read it with students. Then display and read "America's Favorite Shoe." Ask students to identify similarities and differences between the two pieces.

2. Remind students that a fact is something that can be proven and an opinion expresses the writer's thoughts or beliefs and cannot be proven.

3. Help students determine that the first essay mainly expresses opinion. The second essay expresses an opinion that is supported by facts. Point out that an opinion essay is improved by including facts that support the writer's point of view.

4. Have students note that the writer of "America's Favorite Shoe" began the essay by stating an opinion and then provided facts to support that opinion. Invite student volunteers to identify the opinions in the piece by underlining them in one color. Have them underline the facts used to support the opinions in another color. Mention that writers sometimes provide facts first and then state an opinion based on those facts.

5. Suggest a current classroom, school, or community issue. Ask students to jot down an opinion about the issue. Group students with similar opinions about the issue. Give groups three minutes to brainstorm supporting facts for their opinions. Provide time for sharing.

Assessment Connection

Review students' essays to determine whether students have supported their opinions with appropriate facts. Conduct individual conferences with students who are having difficulty distinguishing facts from opinions. Ask them to bring to the conference a piece of writing that expresses an opinion. Have them identify the opinions and the facts in the same way the class completed the exercise in #4 under Teaching the Lesson.

Practicing the Skill

- Ask each student to use the topic from the group work or select another issue and draft an opinion essay supported with facts.

- Read selected pages from books that have opinions expressed from various contributors. Two very good examples are *Boys Know It All* and *Girls Know Best,* both compiled by Michelle Roehm. Ask students to determine whether the opinions you read are supported by facts.

- Have students examine letters to the editor in a local newspaper. Have them identify the letter writer's opinion statements and supporting details.

Blackline Masters

Writing samples, which are models for types of writing, accompany some of the Mini-lessons on blackline masters for students to plan with and refer to as they write.

Writing an Essay: Identifying Facts and Opinions

You Will Need

- transparency markers
- overhead projector
- overhead transparencies of BLM 34 and BLM 34A ("The Case for Sneakers" and "America's Favorite Shoe")
- a collection of books that have opinions expressed by several contributors such as ones compiled by Michelle Roehm

Lesson Background

Students are constantly sharing opinions on many subjects. They also express their views in writing. This mini-lesson helps students understand the difference between fact and opinion and the need to support their viewpoints with factual details.

Teaching the Lesson

1. Display "The Case for Sneakers" on the overhead projector and read it with students. Then display and read "America's Favorite Shoe." Ask students to identify similarities and differences between the two pieces.

2. Remind students that a fact is something that can be proven and an opinion expresses the writer's thoughts or beliefs and cannot be proven.

3. Help students determine that the first essay mainly expresses opinion. The second essay expresses an opinion that is supported by facts. Point out that an opinion essay is improved by including facts that support the writer's point of view.

4. Have students note that the writer of "America's Favorite Shoe" began the essay by stating an opinion and then provided facts to support that opinion. Invite student volunteers to identify the opinions in the piece by underlining them in one color. Have them underline the facts used to support the opinions in another color. Mention that writers sometimes provide facts first and then state an opinion based on those facts.

5. Suggest a current classroom, school, or community issue. Ask students to jot down an opinion about the issue. Group students with similar opinions about the issue. Give groups three minutes to brainstorm supporting facts for their opinions. Provide time for sharing.

Practicing the Skill

- Ask each student to use the topic from the group work or select another issue and draft an opinion essay supported with facts.

- Read selected pages from books that have opinions expressed from various contributors. Two very good examples are *Boys Know It All* and *Girls Know Best*, both compiled by Michelle Roehm. Ask students to determine whether the opinions you read are supported by facts.

- Have students examine letters to the editor in a local newspaper. Have them identify the letter writer's opinion statements and supporting details.

Assessment Connection

Review students' essays to determine whether students have supported their opinions with appropriate facts. Conduct individual conferences with students who are having difficulty distinguishing facts from opinions. Ask them to bring to the conference a piece of writing that expresses an opinion. Have them identify the opinions and the facts in the same way the class completed the exercise in #4 under Teaching the Lesson.

74   Mini-lesson 34

Teaching the Lesson

Your role as teacher is to invite and support your students as they share in a common writing experience as clearly defined in each lesson. Suggestions for beginning the lesson may include discussing an author, sharing writing samples, and/or explaining a writing skill, strategy, or technique. A *Literature* icon indicates where books are used as writing models to foster the reading and writing connection. The detailed Mini-lessons provide explicit suggestions for modeling, questioning, and encouraging students to share their thoughts about each step of writing. An *On Your Own* icon indicates a connection to link the content of the Mini-lesson with students' independent writing.

Writing an Essay: Identifying Facts and Opinions

You Will Need

- transparency markers
- overhead projector
- overhead transparencies of BLM 34 and BLM 34A ("The Case for Sneakers" and "America's Favorite Shoe")
- a collection of books that have opinions expressed by several contributors such as ones compiled by Michelle Roehm

Lesson Background

Students are constantly sharing opinions on many subjects. They also express their views in writing. This mini-lesson helps students understand the difference between fact and opinion and the need to support their viewpoints with factual details.

Teaching the Lesson

1. Display "The Case for Sneakers" on the overhead projector and read it with students. Then display and read "America's Favorite Shoe." Ask students to identify similarities and differences between the two pieces.

2. Remind students that a fact is something that can be proven and an opinion expresses the writer's thoughts or beliefs and cannot be proven.

3. Help students determine that the first essay mainly expresses opinion. The second essay expresses an opinion that is supported by facts. Point out that an opinion essay is improved by including facts that support the writer's point of view.

4. Have students note that the writer of "America's Favorite Shoe" began the essay by stating an opinion and then provided facts to support that opinion. Invite student volunteers to identify the opinions in the piece by underlining them in one color. Have them underline the facts used to support the opinions in another color. Mention that writers sometimes provide facts first and then state an opinion based on those facts.

5. Suggest a current classroom, school, or community issue. Ask students to jot down an opinion about the issue. Group students with similar opinions about the issue. Give groups three minutes to brainstorm supporting facts for their opinions. Provide time for sharing.

Practicing the Skill

- Ask each student to use the topic from the group work or select another issue and draft an opinion essay supported with facts.

- Read selected pages from books that have opinions expressed from various contributors. Two very good examples are *Boys Know It All* and *Girls Know Best*, both compiled by Michelle Roehm. Ask students to determine whether the opinions you read are supported by facts.

- Have students examine letters to the editor in a local newspaper. Have them identify the letter writer's opinion statements and supporting details.

Assessment Connection

Review students' essays to determine whether students have supported their opinions with appropriate facts. Conduct individual conferences with students who are having difficulty distinguishing facts from opinions. Ask them to bring to the conference a piece of writing that expresses an opinion. Have them identify the opinions and the facts in the same way the class completed the exercise in #4 under Teaching the Lesson.

Written Language Development Checklist

Writing Process Checklist

Practicing the Skill

The writing skills, strategies, and techniques that are introduced in the *Teaching the Lesson* section are reinforced to ensure that students retain and apply their learning when they write independently. Ideas for revisiting the lesson in future sessions are included along with additional practice.

Assessment Connection

This section highlights specific skills and strategies for evaluating students' writing samples and behavior during the lessons. For more formal assessment, forms are provided on pages 173–180 of this guide.

Wonder Writers Mini-lessons show you how to model techniques that will help students manage their writing both creatively and logistically.

Prewriting

Writers have to think when they plan their writing. During prewriting, writers generate ideas, decide on a topic, determine their writing purpose, and consider the audience for their writing. Writers select the genre and format of their writing pieces. With the *Prewriting* Mini-lessons, students learn how to make these prewriting decisions.

Students explore different techniques for generating ideas based on their own lives, the literature they read, and their observations of the world. They plan for writing and practice ways to organize their ideas on paper. Students should be invited to venture into many different kinds of writing and to choose new formats for writing. As you honor students' choices, they will take ownership of their writing from the beginning of the writing process.

Drafting

Writers develop their own unique ways of getting started on a writing project. They bring their interests, knowledge of chosen topics, experiences with written language, and reading experiences to the process. As they begin writing, they also learn what else they may need to find out about the topic, the structures and conventions of written language, and the features of the genres and formats in which they are planning to write.

During the *Drafting* Mini-lessons, students learn to view drafting as a way to get started, a time to focus on thoughts and ideas, and a safe place to learn about written language. To guide students as they begin to draft, these Mini-lessons introduce the logistics of writing as well as creative concepts.

By observing and conferencing with students as they are drafting, you will be able to identify relevant learning needs and select from Mini-lessons that teach appropriate capitalization, punctuation, spelling, and grammar skills. As students move further into their writing projects, these Mini-lessons help them organize and develop the flow of their ideas. The draft becomes a real working copy, not just a "step" in the writing process.

The *Wonder Writers* Mini-lessons are organized into five sections according to the steps of the writing process.

See pages 41–48 for the **Prewriting** Mini-lessons.

See pages 49–86 for the **Drafting** Mini-lessons.

Revising

Writers learn as they read, share, and evaluate their writing. They ask themselves questions as they review and revise their pieces. Writers take time to reflect on the content of the message they are working hard to communicate. They also read for clarity and accuracy, and to make sure others can understand their writing, too. Writers need time to share, ask questions, and process responses as they work with their peers and with you.

The **Wonder Writers** *Revising* Mini-lessons for *Content* help students learn how to solicit input from others and to look critically at their own writing. Students share their works-in-progress with a peer or a group, listening to each other and asking questions of one another. With the Mini-lessons, students focus on editing for content to make their writing richer and clearer, which will ultimately help them find their own voices as writers.

See pages 87–95 for the **Revising (Content)** Mini-lessons.

The *Revising* Mini-lessons for *Mechanics* direct students as they edit their work for specific capitalization and punctuation skills, sentence structure, and spelling. As students read, reflect, and share, they realize the power revision has to improve their writing and empower them as individuals with valuable ideas worth sharing and preserving.

See pages 96–99 for the **Revising (Mechanics)** Mini-lessons.

Publishing

The *Publishing* Mini-lessons invite young writers to become contributing members of the literacy community in your classroom and beyond. Students review their own pieces to decide if they want to publish and how they want to publish. After writers choose the pieces they want to publish, they polish their work and craft a finished product. Sharing a finished piece becomes a celebration for the author and for the classroom.

See pages 100–102 for the **Publishing** Mini-lessons.

Assessment

If students are truly to view themselves as writers, it is important that they monitor their own progress. This makes them conscious of their successes and invested in improving their skills. These practical suggestions help students take ownership of their writing and strive for independence as writers.

See pages 103–104 for the **Assessment** Mini-lessons.

About the Writing Strategy Cards

The *Wonder Writers* Writing Strategy Cards are a unique and exciting innovation in writing instruction. Taking writing instruction beyond prewriting and the conventions of writing—spelling, grammar, and mechanics—the Writing Strategy Cards help students understand how successful writers think throughout the writing process.

The Writing Strategy Cards help students learn to think like writers and see themselves as writers as they explore different types of writing for different purposes. The 32 Writing Strategy Cards (16 two-sided cards) at the Grade 5 level serve as a resource for the students and for you. They highlight real-world connections to specific strategies used by all writers, regardless of experience or expertise.

Each Writing Strategy Card showcases a single writing strategy on an attractive poster to engage writers. The cards are organized under five broad categories: Writers Write What They Know; Writers Collect Words, Ideas, and Other Things; Writers Don't Give Up; Writers Write for Many Reasons; and Writers Like to Learn. You may choose to select specific lessons as needed to meet the needs of the writers in your classroom. Each Writing Strategy Card has corresponding Teacher Notes in the *Teacher's Writers Resource* to help you present the strategy. A reproducible Student Activity Page follows each teacher's page so students can practice the strategy. You may present the strategy cards to small groups or to the whole class.

Writing Strategy Cards

Writers Write What They Know
- Writers write about people. #17
- Writers write about things that are important to them. #23
- Writers write about special moments. #19 ◄
- Writers write about the unexpected and unusual. #21
- Writers remember the past. #3
- Writers are all different. #24

> Writers tap into their own worlds to discover their topics. They establish ownership of their writing.

Writers Collect Words, Ideas, and Other Things
- Writers are readers. #11
- Writers notice little things. #20
- Writers collect ideas. #25 ◄
- Writers collect writing they like. #7
- Writers investigate and collect facts. #14
- Writers are people-watchers and good listeners. #5

> Writers make connections between their reading, their writing, and their lives. They discover their passions as they connect and collect.

Writers Don't Give Up
- Writers aren't always inspired. #13
- Writers don't always start at the beginning. #26
- Writers get help. #29
- Writers reread and rewrite. #22 ◄
- Writers get to the point. #9

> Writers solve problems and learn from their revisions as they craft their work. They understand that writing doesn't have to be perfect and that rethinking their writing is part of the process.

Writers Write for Many Reasons
- Writers write with a purpose. #10
- Writers write for their readers. #30
- Writers are storytellers. #15
- Writers are reporters. #31
- Writers are poets. #6
- Writers send messages. #32
- Writers explain. #2 ◄
- Writers describe. #27
- Writers persuade. #12
- Writers solve problems. #1

> Writers explore their craft and their world as they write for different purposes and for different audiences.

Writers Like to Learn
- Writers are curious. #8
- Writers daydream and imagine. #28
- Writers learn from other writers. #16 ◄
- Writers wonder. #18
- Writers experiment. #4

> Writers explore, research, and imagine to create their writing. They know that they learn when they read and write.

Writers are all different.

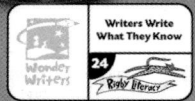

Writers Write
What They Know

24

Wonder Writers

Rigby Literacy

© 2003 Rigby Photograph: Bill Burlingham

A suggested teaching order for the Writing Strategy Cards helps you link reading and writing skills and strategies with those taught in the *Rigby Literacy Comprehension Quarterlies.*

Writing Strategy Teacher Notes

The Writing Strategy Teacher Notes help define the featured writing strategy and present suggestions for reinforcing the strategy with students. As students practice each strategy, they will learn about themselves as writers and understand how to connect the strategy to their own writing. The activities are carefully designed to move the instructional focus gradually from the card to real-world writing.

A concise introduction defines the strategy and explains why it is important to writers.

Writers Write What They Know

Writers are all different.

Literature Connection
- *26 Fairmount Avenue* by Tomie dePaola
- *A Long Way from Chicago: A Novel in Stories* by Richard Peck
- *Joey Pigza Loses Control* by Jack Gantos
- *What a Writer Needs* by Ralph Fletcher

Teacher Tip
On the following Student Activity Page students are asked to rewrite a journal entry for others to read and then to write about a meaningful topic in their own voice. Before students begin writing, discuss the concept of "voice" in writing as one's unique way of expressing thoughts and feelings. Stress the importance of writing with voice by contrasting different authors' styles.

Writers are unique, bringing different experiences and ways of thinking to their work. Since no two people are the same, good writers work hard at developing their own voices, writing about their own backgrounds, interests, and experiences, and making their writing direct, personal, and honest.

Making the Connection
- Ask students to look at the card. How does the illustration reflect the difference of writers? Students should note that, although there are similarities among all the people in the picture, it's easy to see that each student has unique interests. One plays violin, one skates, one paints and plays baseball, and so on.
- Explain that just as people have different interests, they also have individual and unique ways of thinking, speaking, and writing. In writing, an individual's "voice" is not only what he or she says but also *how* he or she says it. Writing with your own voice is honest and open; it lets the reader know who you are—in the same way an observer knows which student in the picture loves cheerleading and which one never leaves home without his skateboard.

Connecting to Real Life
- Read aloud excerpts from books with distinctive voices. You might choose *26 Fairmount Avenue* by Tomie dePaola, *A Long Way from Chicago: A Novel in Stories* by Richard Peck, or *Joey Pigza Loses Control* by Jack Gantos. Discuss how the authors use voice in each.
- Explore with students the differences in voice, and how each writer's unique writing is lively, believable, and powerful.
- Share the quotation, "Writing *with voice* is writing into which someone has breathed" (Peter Elbow, quoted by Fletcher in *What a Writer Needs,* Chapter 6). Together, discuss what this idea might mean.

Just for You
Voltaire said, "I don't agree with a word you say, but I will defend to the death your right to say it." While most would argue that this quotation is a reflection on freedom of speech, it could apply to voice also. Do you read books and stories with a lot of different voices? Do you try to write in different voices?

Making the Connection presents *suggestions* for introducing the writing strategy to students. The Writing Strategy Card is a springboard for the discussion of the featured strategy and how student writers can use the strategy.

Connecting to Real Life presents authentic examples of how the strategy is relevant to student writing and to the writing of familiar authors as students make literature connections. The engaging activities invite students to practice the strategy on their own.

Just for You addresses teachers as writers, with insightful, reflective questions and ideas. Interesting information about authors and writing is often included.

Student Activity Pages

The Student Activity Pages present engaging activities that go beyond what's been taught with the Writing Strategy Cards. Students learn to connect the strategy with what they do in their own writing and with what "real" authors do. The Student Activity Pages can be done in small groups, whole groups, or independently. Students may use the information on the Student Activity Pages as a reference as they work on their various writing pieces.

The introduction explains and personalizes the strategy for students in a way that helps them connect it to their own lives.

Specific techniques for using the strategy help students make a connection between the strategy, their own lives, and their writing.

Varied ideas for writing and using the strategy help students make connections with their own lives and "real" authors. Many of the writing ideas involve discussing writing topics and thoughts with friends and family members. Many references to literature and book titles, authors' personal experiences, and excerpts from literature provide examples of the strategies being used in the "real world."

Name _____ Date _____

Writers are all different.

There's no one else like you! You're a special individual with your own interests and experiences. Let your writing reflect the real you. Make your writing lively, honest, and powerful by writing in your own voice.

Let the World Hear Your Voice!

Ralph Fletcher says that one purpose of keeping a journal is to "provide a place to relax, to settle into a comfortable writing stride." He speaks about his "easy journal voice," which is relaxed because he is the sole audience. Then he tries to let some of his easy journal voice "leak into" the writing he does for publication (*What a Writer Needs*).

1. **Choose an entry in your writer's notebook that is written in your "easy journal voice."**
2. **Then rewrite the entry for others to read. You may edit and polish as necessary, but don't remove your voice! Remember to let your personal voice "leak into" your writing for readers to enjoy.**

If You Wouldn't Say It . . .

To help students understand voice, Mike Brusko says, "If you wouldn't say it that way, don't write it that way" (*Writing Rules!*). Write like you talk, and write about things you enjoy and know well.

1. **Choose a writing topic that is meaningful to you. Or choose a story idea that is based on a personal, memorable experience.**
2. **As you work, occasionally read your words aloud. Does the writing sound natural and lively? Is it in your own voice?**

Writer's Handbook

The *Writer's Handbook* is a valuable, usable, and engaging reference book for both teachers and students. As students become more independent, they need to use reference books to answer their questions about spelling, capitalization, grammar, and usage. The writing skills covered in the *Writer's Handbook* are appropriate for Grades 4 and 5.

Table of Contents

Introduction

Questions about writing pop up all the time, and we don't always have the answers. When do I capitalize the word **mother?** What's the correct abbreviation for **ounce?** All is not lost if you don't know the answer. All you really need to know is where to look.

The Writer's Handbook is just the place to look for all kinds of answers. It covers rules for questions about spelling, capitalization, punctuation, and grammar. Think of **The Writer's Handbook** as a place to find answers.

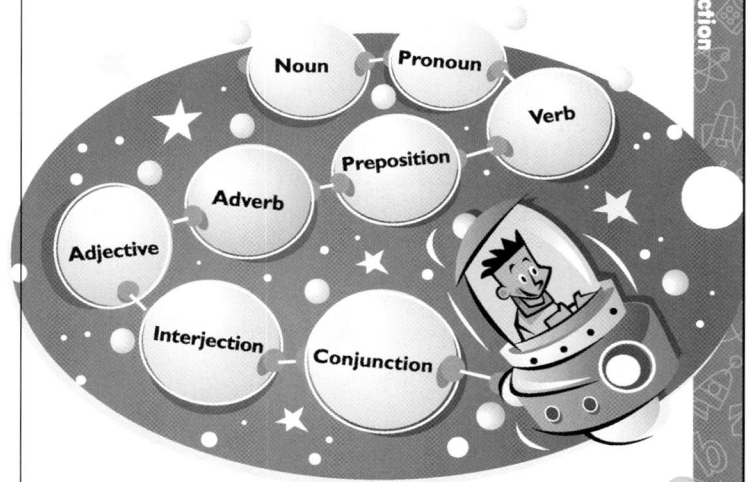

The *Writer's Handbook* is:
- for students as they do content-area writing in Writer's Workshop or as they work on projects as a group or independently;
- for teachers to use as they prepare Mini-lessons on grammar, usage, and mechanics during Writer's Workshop or language arts block.

Punctuation

As you write, do you ever wonder where to place a comma or when to start a new sentence? You may know many of the rules of punctuation. After all, you punctuate your speech whenever you talk to someone. Read the examples below and see just how important correct punctuation can be.

Without punctuation:

Keisha was worried about her test she had a basketball game that afternoon and the team was counting on her to play well Keisha would have to be rested calm and relaxed she would definitely have to be happy with her test score.

With punctuation:

Keisha was worried about her test. She had a basketball game that afternoon, and the team was counting on her. To play well, Keisha would have to be rested, calm, and relaxed. She would definitely have to be happy with her test score.

You can easily learn the basics of punctuation. Read on to find out more!

Periods ●

Use a period to end a sentence and to mark abbreviations, initials, and decimal points.

At the End of a Sentence

Joe's birthday party lasted well past midnight.

After Abbreviations

Dr., Mrs., Mr., Ph.D., etc., vs., ex., A.M., P.M.

Use only one period when an abbreviation marks the end of a sentence.

Our teacher uses the title of Ms.

After Initials

C. S. Lewis

Booker T. Washington

As a Decimal

Don's temperature was a feverish 101.1 degrees.

Isabel was shortchanged by $1.50 at the store.

eggs , bacon , and bread .

The *Writer's Handbook* provides clear definitions of writing vocabulary accompanied by writing examples.

Tips give extra bits of useful and interesting information to young writers.

Commas ,

Commas help the reader know where to pause. Use a comma to break up words and ideas, and to keep sentences clear. Commas are essential in the following situations:

Items in a Series

Use a comma to separate words, phrases, or clauses in a series.

Words: **My mom picked up eggs, bacon, and bread at the grocery store.**

Phrases: **Sean enjoys playing basketball, hiking in the mountains, and riding horses.**

In Dates and Addresses

Use a comma to separate items in dates and addresses.

Date: **The Declaration of Independence was signed on July 4, 1776.**

Address: **Audrey's new address is 1200 Montview Street, Denver, Colorado 80207.**

To Set Off Dialogue

Use a comma to distinguish the words of a speaker from the rest of the sentence.

The boxer Muhammad Ali said, "I am the greatest."

Do not use a comma when you are merely reporting what someone said.

Jake said the test was easy.

In Direct Address

Use a comma to separate a noun of direct address (the person to whom one is speaking) from the rest of the sentence.

Alonso, don't eat so much right before dinner!

In Letter Writing

Use a comma after the greeting and closing in friendly letters.

Greeting: **Dear Grandpa Leo,**

Closing: **With love,**

Tip

In business letters, use a *colon* (:) after the greeting.

Dear Rigby:

Writing in a Balanced Literacy Classroom

A balanced literacy Grade 5 classroom is built upon a supportive learning environment. Students read, write, speak, listen, and observe through authentic literacy experiences:

- The diverse lives, personalities, and learning needs of each student are valued and respected.

- Students are immersed in many types of books and print.

- All students are viewed as learners and view themselves as learners.

- Students learn to read, write, and work together as well as individually.

- There is time for practicing, sharing, and responding.

- Students' voices are heard as they make reading and writing choices and take steps toward becoming independent learners.

Wonder Writers is designed to engage students and teachers in real-life writing experiences within balanced literacy. The developmentally appropriate Grade 5 Mini-lessons, Writing Strategy Cards, and Student Activity Pages are built upon the strengths of learners at this grade level and are designed to accommodate varying instructional levels and learning styles. Students will make important reading and writing connections through the literacy experiences provided in *Wonder Writers.* As a reflective teacher, you are encouraged to model and share yourself as a writer and reader as well—*Wonder Writers* will show you how!

Each of the balanced literacy approaches—*modeled, shared, guided, interactive,* and *independent*—involve different degrees of learner responsibility and teacher support. Learning experiences are structured to occur in independent, small, and whole groups for flexibility. The reflective, skilled teacher weighs this "balance" of literacy experiences, student/teacher responsibility, and small-group/whole-group instruction to plan curriculum and support students as they move toward independence. Through careful observation and assessment, you can learn the unique strengths and needs of the students in your classroom, who will undoubtedly be at different stages of language development.

When you do a Mini-lesson, present a Writing Strategy Card, or introduce a Student Activity Page, the instructional approach you use will depend on students' previous writing experiences, their level of literacy development, and their ability to work together cooperatively. At the beginning of the year and when introducing particularly challenging skills and strategies, you may want to use *modeled writing*. As students grow in their literacy development and as a community of writers, you may prefer to use more *shared* and *guided writing*. Striking the right balance among the approaches may vary from group to group and from year to year. As the primary observer of students' literacy development in your classroom, the decisions for releasing responsibility must ultimately be up to you.

Using Read-Alouds and Think-Alouds as Models

Reading aloud to students models fluent reading and introduces writers to a new world of books. Reading many different kinds of books provides a wider variety of models for students' future writing. **Wonder Writers** Mini-lessons, Writing Strategy Cards, and Student Activity Pages suggest a variety of quality trade book titles for reading aloud. Sharing aloud your thoughts, feelings, and observations while you read and write further helps students understand the writing process. **Wonder Writers** Mini-lessons encourage you to share your thoughts with students. Think-aloud prompts are provided to help you focus on features of the text, vocabulary, author's style, text organization, sentence structure, and writing strategies.

Using Modeled Writing

In modeled writing, you demonstrate the writing process by thinking aloud while composing a text on the board or on chart paper. In this approach, you introduce students to a variety of writing forms. As you write, you show students that composing a text requires thought and presents challenges. A modeled writing session should focus on a brief piece of writing related to the learning experiences in the classroom. In **Wonder Writers,** modeled writing is used in the Mini-lessons to show students how you make decisions about content, punctuation, spelling, grammar, vocabulary, text style, and format.

Tips for Reading Aloud

- Select books that interest students.
- Always practice reading the book and doing a think-aloud before reading to students.
- Keep the read-aloud book in the classroom to help students make reading and writing connections. The book can then be conveniently used as a familiar writing model.

Teaching Tip

A Mini-lesson should only last from 10 to 20 minutes. Keep the modeled writing short and focused on the skill or strategy featured in the Mini-lesson.

Using Shared Writing and Interactive Writing

Shared Writing

During shared writing sessions, you serve as the scribe as you work together with students to compose and then read a text. The primary responsibility for composing the text lies with students—you contribute by sharing ideas and pointing out the use of strategies. As you write, you encourage students to share their thinking. The content of the writing may connect with a shared or guided reading experience or another classroom event. The teaching focus may include conventions of print, strategies for spelling, writing process, writing style, and text organization. In *Wonder Writers,* shared writing is used to learn about the writing process and writing strategies while exploring different types of writing.

Interactive Writing

During interactive writing, which should naturally evolve from shared writing, teacher and students interact to compose an accurate text. Unlike shared writing, students assume a more active role by holding the pen and by doing the actual writing. You provide explicit instruction at the "teachable" moment. Student writing may be kept and used as a sample for documenting their writing development. Interactive writing serves as a way to explicitly teach and practice specific writing and spelling skills.

Using Guided Writing

Guided writing is writing by students, with guidance and instruction from you. In this student-centered workshop, students work as a community of learners who support one another through sharing and responding. Although students may select their own topics, their writing pieces may also be an extension of an independent, guided, or shared reading experience. As students are writing, you may meet with individual students and confer with them about relevant writing process issues, skills, strategies, and content.

Teaching Tip

To establish ownership and identify writers, have each student use a different colored ink when contributing to the text of an interactive activity.

In *Wonder Writers,* guided writing is used to guide, share, respond and extend students' thinking strategies as they practice the writing process and become more independent.

A Framework for Guided Writing

Whole-Group Mini-lesson or Writing Strategy Card Lesson (10-20 minutes)

The whole class meets for a short, focused lesson, which may— but does not have to—relate to a shared or guided reading lesson. The topic of the lesson is determined by the needs of students. *Wonder Writers* Mini-lessons and Writing Strategy Cards, which may relate to writing process, style, or writing conventions, provide the focus of the whole-group session.

Individual Writing and Conferences (20-30 minutes)

Students work independently on their pieces as you circulate, observe, and confer with individuals about their writing. You continue to reinforce the Mini-lesson or Writing Strategy Card content as you conference with students individually.

Whole-Group Sharing (10-15 minutes)

The class gathers together as you facilitate a whole-group sharing to listen and respond to a writer's piece and reinforce the Mini-lesson or Writing Strategy Card focus.

Using Independent Writing

Independent writing empowers writers to explore the craft of writing and is the ultimate goal of all writing instruction. Just as we teach reading to create independent, lifelong readers, we should meet the challenge of teaching writing with the same goal. The writing ideas and extensions within **Wonder Writers** Mini-lessons, Writing Strategy Cards, and Student Activity Pages invite students to explore new types of writing. Students may write about relevant curriculum topics and classroom learning experiences, about the books they have read, or reflective personal pieces. The skills and strategies they learn with **Wonder Writers** will increase their mastery of writing and their confidence in themselves as writers.

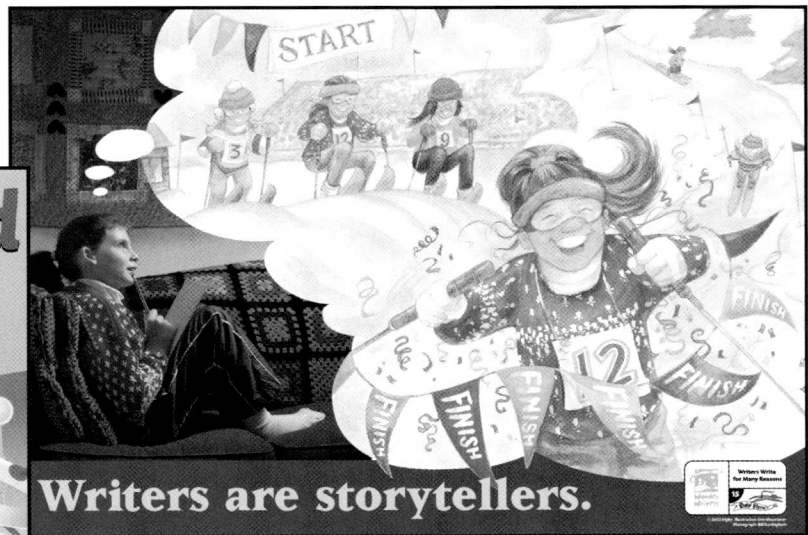

Writing and Spelling Development

Young students are busy thinkers as they learn to write. They wonder about what to write, puzzle about how to write and spell words, and question how to organize their writing. They explore the world of print as they write, draw, review, and talk about their writing to make and maintain meaning. Within the supportive literacy experiences launched by **Wonder Writers,** students learn to develop a sense of purpose for their writing, how to consider their audience, and how to express their own voices.

While students are engaged in authentic writing experiences within **Wonder Writers,** your task is to observe their use of writing strategies, skills, and behaviors. Students' writing samples provide valuable insight into their specific developmental traits. In your classroom, students may be at different stages of writing and spelling development, yet the **Wonder Writers** Mini-lessons, Writing Strategy Cards, and Student Activity Pages are appropriate for all students since they present strategies that all writers use and spend lifetimes perfecting.

The purpose of assessing writing is to discover where each individual student falls on a chart of development. Knowing this helps you determine what he or she needs to learn to continue to grow as a writer. Building the specific instructional experiences that will take students to this next level of growth then becomes an informed, purposeful process.

This chart provides seven areas of development for you to focus on as you plan instruction and assess your students' writing. You can use this chart, "Snapshots" of Student Writers on pages 28 and 29, the assessment forms on pages 173–180, and the *Assessment Connections* in the Mini-lessons to help you assess the writing ability of the students in your classroom.

Fluent Written Language Development Chart

Planning

- Selects writing forms for specific purposes and audiences
- Makes lists and notes about ideas
- Demonstrates knowledge of topic
- Maintains a central idea or single focus
- Presents information in a logical sequence
- Creates a "voice"
- Adds depth and description with the five senses
- Attempts a variety of fiction and nonfiction writing such as: historical fiction, adventure, mystery, science fiction, humor, fantasy, realistic, expository, poetry, tall tales, fairy tales, persuasive, formal letter, personal narrative, narrative, and instructions

Use the *Prewriting* Mini-lessons and the Writing Strategy Cards to help students select their topics and genres, determine their purpose, and address different audiences.

Content and Message

- Develops beginning, middle, and ending
- Uses complete sentences and recognizes correct word order
- Demonstrates an understanding of subject-verb agreement
- Builds and organizes paragraphs effectively
- Writes grammatically correct complex sentences
- Uses varied sentence beginnings and endings
- Uses multiple adjectives to describe something
- Uses alliteration, onomatopoeia, and other figures of speech
- Develops characters through thoughts, feelings, and actions
- Defines setting
- Makes transitions in time, setting, and point of view

continued . . .

Use the *Drafting* and *Revising (Content)* Mini-lessons and the Writing Strategy Cards to help your students with grammar, syntax, punctuation, spelling, and vocabulary.

Fluent Written Language Development Chart
(continued)

Punctuation

- Uses basic capitalization and punctuation rules
- Has an awareness of commas, exclamation marks, and question marks
- Uses commas, exclamation marks, and question marks correctly

Spelling

- Makes many close approximations
- Marks approximations for checking
- Uses reference materials to check spelling
- Writes more correct spellings than approximations
- Uses inflected endings *-ed, -ing, -s* correctly

Vocabulary

- Uses adjectives and adverbs
- Makes comparisons using similes and metaphors
- Experiments with new vocabulary

continued . . .

Fluent Written Language Development Chart
(continued)

Editing

- Uses a variety of revising strategies
- Uses correct marks for revising text
- Revises to improve progression and clarity of ideas
- Revises to include more descriptive and sensory details
- Attempts several spellings of a word
- Marks words to check
- Rereads text to check for sense

Computer

- Knows the basic keyboard
- Uses editing keys and functions
- Makes deletions
- Makes insertions
- Makes corrections
- Manipulates text on the screen
- Uses a spell-check feature if available
- Saves
- Prints

Use the *Revising (Mechanics)* Mini-lessons and the Writing Strategy Cards to help your students with the accuracy required for publication.

"Snapshots" of Student Writers

Writing samples from your students are powerful indicators of students' writing development. An analysis of writing samples gives you a "snapshot" of the student as a writer. You can see the student's stage of understanding text composition and use of writing conventions and strategies. These snapshots capture the level of performance that is in turn used to assess the student's writing development. After collecting a writer snapshot, you can use *Wonder Writer* Mini-lessons and Writing Strategy Cards as part of your instructional plan.

Knowing what to look for in a writing sample is key to its value for assessment. This Grade 5 writing sample is an example of writing about a topic with two different genres: poetry and narrative.

Writing Sample Assessment:
- Chooses to write in a variety of genres: poetry and narrative
- Develops beginning, middle, and end
- Defines setting

Wonder Writers Mini-lessons could focus on:
- Drafting: Language and Word Choice (16)
- Drafting: Developing a Character Through Thoughts, Feelings, and Actions (19)
- Revising: Checking Spelling (59)

Possible **Wonder Writers** Writing Strategy Card: Writers write about special moments. (19)

A Mud Puddle

A mud puddle
My mother warned me
It will come below my feet
By the wheat tree.

A puddle I did fall in
And landed on my face
I was muddy head to toe
Oh was I a disgrace!

A mud puddle
My mother warned me
Father was filming it
For everyone to see.

This nersery ryhme is about a true story that happened to me when I was 4.
My grandparents lived on a farm and raised wheat. One year we went

When gathering writing samples for assessment, be sure to include both teacher-selected and student-selected pieces. Students may keep their own writing folders—which can be used for collecting samples at regular intervals—for routine, ongoing assessment and for checking on specific skills or strategies.

to their house for wheat harvest. While we were out in the fields, my dad was filming the combine eating up the wheat. My mom had dressed me in a pretty pink and white outfit. After we ate lunch I decided to walk around. Forgetting about the warning that my mother had given me about the mud puddles I was off. Happy as I was it ended with a PLOP! I fell into a mud puddle and was covered from head to toe in mud. I was so furious I could have hit somebody. But the funniest part about it was that my dad recorded it all on video.

Assessment of literacy development:
- Has awareness of story structure
- Uses descriptive words
- Maintains a single focus

Wonder Writers Mini-lessons should focus on:
- Checking spelling
- Writing a paragraph
- Writing a long story

Possible *Wonder Writers* Writing Strategy Card: Writers are storytellers. (15)

Stages of English Language Development and Suggested Teaching Strategies

When choosing Mini-lessons and Writing Strategy Cards, the following tips will provide you with help as ESL/ELL students move from stage to stage in their language acquisition and literacy development.

Stage 1: Preproduction

Students in this stage . . .
- respond primarily nonverbally
- display limited comprehension
- manipulate objects or things to communicate
- observe storytelling, shared reading, chanting, and singing
- rely heavily on pictures in shared reading

Suggested Teaching Strategies:
- Modify speech delivery by slowing down, simplifying, enunciating clearly, using gestures and body language, and supporting speech with visual aids.
- Focus primarily on group experiences.
- Lead shared writing activities that rely on picture support and focus on everyday language.
- Select activities that use real-world items students can touch, see, feel, hear, or smell.
- Follow up reading with activities that focus on drama, music and songs, mime, and movement.

> *Goal: Build students' English listening comprehension and vocabulary.*

Stage 2: Early Production

Students in this stage . . .
- use some basic words and simple phrases
- express needs and preferences with routine language expressions
- memorize favorite rhymes, songs, and chants
- manipulate objects or things to communicate
- begin to comprehend storytelling, shared reading, chanting, and singing
- rely heavily on pictures in shared reading
- participate in guided reading only when used in a shared reading manner
- participate in language-experience situations

Suggested Teaching Strategies:

Use the strategies outlined for Stage 1 and add the following:
- Add group language-experience activities to your writing activities.
- Follow up reading with activities that focus on movement and drawing.
- Actively encourage students to join in a group response or repeated refrain during shared reading.

Stage 3: Speech Emergence

Students in this stage . . .
- participate in everyday conversations about familiar topics
- produce longer, complete phrases and sentences with errors that still hinder comprehension
- display increasing comprehension
- actively participate in shared reading/writing and guided reading
- rely on high-frequency words and known language patterns in shared reading
- participate in heavily scaffolded guided writing with strong teacher support
- begin to approximate independent reading

Suggested Teaching Strategies:
- Speak at a normal pace while simplifying, enunciating clearly, using gestures, and sometimes supporting speech with visual aids.
- Follow shared writing suggestions outlined for Stages 1 and 2.
- Scaffold collaborative and individual writing by providing prewriting activities that include pictures and graphic organizers such as semantic webs.
- Select activities linked to, but no longer driven by, real-world items.
- Focus primarily on group experiences.

Goal: Continue building students' vocabulary while motivating them to produce the vocabulary they know.

Goal: Continue building students' vocabulary while building higher levels of language use.

Stage 4: Intermediate Fluency

Students in this stage . . .
- engage in ordinary conversations with more complex sentences and phrases
- make errors that no longer hinder comprehension
- begin to use multiple strategies to construct meaning from print
- actively participate in shared reading/writing, guided reading/writing, and independent reading

Suggested Teaching Strategies:
- Use normal speech, supporting academic language with visual aids.
- Incorporate interactive writing activities.
- Provide a variety of individual and group experiences.
- Engage students in meaningful discussions about books.

Goal: Continue building students' vocabulary and higher levels of language use in the content areas.

Stage 5: Advanced Fluency

Students in this stage . . .
- produce language comparable to that of a native speaker
- actively use academic language to negotiate meaning
- use multiple strategies to construct meaning from print
- actively participate in all areas of balanced literacy, both reading and writing

Suggested Teaching Strategies:
- Use normal speech, supporting academic language with visual aids.

Goal: Continue building students' literacy learning and academic language according to grade-level expectations.

Assessment in *Wonder Writers*

Wonder Writers includes a variety of techniques and tools to assess student progress. Opportunity for assessment is provided during Mini-lessons, with students' writing samples, within the writing workshop, and in teacher/student conferences.

Assessment Connections

In the Mini-lessons, the *Assessment Connections* highlight specific skills and strategies for assessing student's writing and behaviors during the lessons.

Assessment Tools and Techniques

The following assessment tools, which are on pages 173–181, can be used to organize and document the information gathered from students.

Ongoing Assessment Record

The assessment record suggests a time frame for reading and writing assessments. Gathering data at scheduled intervals will help create a complete picture of the individual's reading and writing development. Refer to the Ongoing Assessment Record on page 173.

Student Interview

A student interview will help you assess the student's writing interests and instructional needs. Interviews can be done during teacher-led conferences. Refer to the Student Interview on pages 174–175.

Written Language Development Checklist

Writing expectations are grade-level appropriate and are included in the writing development checklist. Refer to the Written Language Development Checklist on pages 176–177.

Writing Process Checklist

Anecdotal records, writing samples, and writing conferences will provide you with the data necessary to keep a writing process checklist for each of your writers. Refer to the Writing Process Checklist on page 178.

Creating Writing Rubrics

Rubrics can be specifically designed to focus on writing skills or strategies. Refer to Creating Writing Rubrics on page 179.

Student Writing Portfolios

Portfolios should include teacher-selected *and* student-selected writing samples. Portfolios are a comprehensive collection of a student's written language development. Refer to Student Writing Portfolios on page 180.

Teacher Tips for Writing Conferences

When you conference with students you are teaching them how to assess their own writing strengths and areas for development. The teacher tips help you encourage students to become independent thinkers and writers. Refer to the Teacher Tips for Writing Conferences on page 181.

Rigby Literacy K-5
Scope and Sequence

Phonics, Decoding, and Structural Analysis	K	1	2	3	4	5
Names and identifies letters of the alphabet	■	■	■			
Knows the order of the alphabet	■					
Uses knowledge of letter-sound relationships	■	■				
Develops and applies knowledge of consonant sounds	■	■	■	■	■	■
Develops and applies knowledge of consonant blends	■	■	■	■	■	■
Develops and applies knowledge of consonant digraphs	■	■	■	■	■	■
Develops and applies knowledge of short vowels	■	■	■			
Develops and applies knowledge of long vowels		■	■	■		
Demonstrates understanding of R-controlled vowels		■	■	■	■	■
Uses knowledge of vowel diphthongs		■	■	■	■	■
Uses knowledge of vowel digraphs		■	■	■	■	■
Uses knowledge of vowel variants		■	■	■	■	■
Uses knowledge of word families to decode		■	■	■		
Uses knowledge of syllables to decode multiple-syllable words			■	■	■	■
Uses knowledge of spelling patterns to decode [CVC, CVCe, CV]		■	■	■		
Identifies and reads compound words		■	■	■	■	■
Identifies and reads contractions		■	■	■	■	■
Identifies root words		■	■	■	■	■
Demonstrates understanding of noun plurals	■	■	■	■	■	■
Demonstrates understanding of possessives		■	■	■	■	■
Demonstrates understanding of inflected endings [-ed, -ing, -s]		■	■	■	■	■
Uses knowledge of prefixes			■	■	■	■
Uses knowledge of suffixes			■	■	■	■
Demonstrates understanding of syllabication in words		■	■	■	■	■
Reads simple one-syllable and high-frequency words	■	■				
Reads more complex and irregularly spelled words			■	■	■	■

Comprehension – Uses prior knowledge and experiences / Uses and extends what is known	K	1	2	3	4	5
Activates existing background knowledge / Makes connections with text based on personal experiences and knowledge / Makes connections with text based on educational experience and knowledge	■	■	■	■	■	■
Builds background knowledge / Uses illustrations and text features to help store important new information	■	■	■	■	■	■

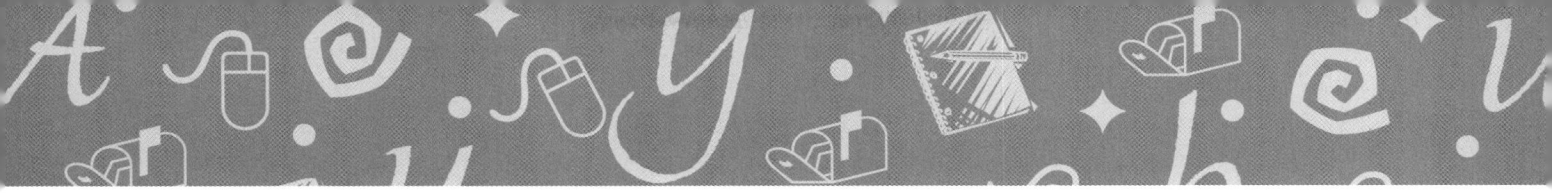

Comprehension – *Determines what is important in text / Determines important ideas and themes*

	K	1	2	3	4	5
Identifies main ideas or themes / Identifies main ideas and supporting details	■	■	■	■	■	■
Utilizes text features and text structures to determine importance / Uses personal beliefs, experiences, and prior learning to determine importance		■	■	■	■	■
Recognizes cause and effect			■	■		
Compares and contrasts information / Classifies and ranks important vs. unimportant information	■	■	■	■	■	
Considers purpose for reading					■	■
Recognizes theme and relevance to reader						■

Comprehension – *Draws inferences / Infers*

	K	1	2	3	4	5
Makes and confirms predictions / Makes, changes, and checks predictions	■	■	■	■	■	■
Draws conclusions		■	■	■		
Makes generalizations			■	■		
Forms and supports opinions			■	■		
Makes critical judgments					■	■
Creates personal interpretation / Forms personal interpretations			■	■	■	■

Comprehension – *Asks questions to confirm understanding / Asks questions*

	K	1	2	3	4	5
Asks questions to clarify meaning / Asks in order to clarify and extend comprehension	■	■	■	■	■	■
Asks questions to understand author		■	■	■		
Asks questions to understand key themes	■	■	■	■		
Asks rhetorical questions			■	■		
Asks in order to preview, plan reading, and predict					■	■
Asks in order to understand how genre influences comprehension					■	■
Asks to recognize and interpret story elements and text features					■	■

Comprehension – *Synthesizes information / Synthesizes*

	K	1	2	3	4	5
Connects ideas from several different sources: text-to-text, text-to-self, text-to-world	■	■	■	■		
Sequences ideas and story events	■	■	■	■		
Summarizes information		■	■	■		
Classifies and categorizes information	■	■	■	■		
Retells story events or key facts / Retells in order to clarify	■	■	■	■	■	■
Considers author's viewpoint, purpose, and style			■	■		
Focuses on text elements to understand overall meaning and theme					■	■
Shares, recommends, and criticizes what's read					■	■

Comprehension – *Uses sensory information / Creates and uses images*

	K	1	2	3	4	5
Creates or uses images from all senses / Makes connections with all 5 senses and with emotions	■	■	■	■	■	■
Visualizes information from text, illustrations, diagrams, etc.	■	■	■	■		

Comprehension – Monitors comprehension	K	1	2	3	4	5
Uses fix-up strategies: *Rereads and reviews text	■	■	■	■	■	■
*Reads on		■	■	■	■	■
*Adjusts pace			■	■	■	■
*Uses decoding, word analysis, syntactic and context clues for word recognition or pronunciation	■	■	■	■	■	■
Self-monitors by asking questions: Does it make sense? Sound right? / Changing your mind as you read	■	■	■	■	■	■

Writing – Applications	K	1	2	3	4	5
Uses labels and captions in writing	■	■				
Retells personal experiences [dictation, language experience]	■	■				
Writes narrative text based on personal experience	■	■	■	■	■	■
Writes narrative text [humorous, realistic, fantasy]		■	■	■	■	■
Writes letters [informal, formal]		■	■	■	■	■
Writes descriptive text [people, places, books]		■	■	■	■	■
Writes expository text [essays, reports, directions, research results]		■	■	■	■	■
Writes persuasive text			■	■	■	■
Demonstrates an awareness of story structure	■	■	■	■		
Includes setting, plot, resolution, and characters in appropriate writing formats				■	■	■
Includes dialogue where appropriate					■	■
Uses more complex literary forms [tall tales, fairy tales, poetry]			■	■	■	■
Uses author's styles as models for improving writing			■	■	■	■
Writes from a variety of points of view					■	■
Demonstrates development of a personal style of writing				■	■	■

Writing – Organization and Focus	K	1	2	3	4	5
Writes to communicate ideas and reflections	■	■	■	■	■	■
Selects writing forms for specific purposes and audiences		■	■	■	■	■
Maintains a central idea or single focus		■	■	■	■	■
Presents information in a logical sequence		■	■	■	■	■
Uses knowledge of regular spelling patterns [CVC; CVCe]		■	■	■		
Uses basic capitalization and punctuation rules		■	■	■	■	■
Writes messages that move left-to-right and top-to-bottom	■	■	■	■		
Uses a variety of simple, compound, and complex sentences				■	■	■
Demonstrates an understanding of the alphabetical principle	■	■	■			
Uses letters and phonetically spelled words	■	■				
Uses orthographic pattern rules	■	■	■	■		
Uses conventional spellings for simple, regularly spelled words		■	■	■		
Uses descriptive words to elaborate on story details			■	■	■	■
Connects related ideas in writing / Demonstrates the ability to develop a topic	■	■	■	■	■	■
Uses topic sentences with supporting sentences in writing				■	■	■

Writing – Organization and Focus continued	K	1	2	3	4	5
Incorporates simple transitions in writing / Writes with a distinct beginning, middle, end			■	■	■	■
Uses paragraphs effectively in writing / Groups sentences with related information into paragraphs				■	■	■
Uses titles and headings that are appropriate to the writing				■	■	■

Writing – Evaluation and Revision	K	1	2	3	4	5
Uses a variety of prewriting strategies [draw, talk, map, KWL, Venn diagram, brainstorm, notes, lists, diagrams]	■	■	■	■	■	
Uses a variety of revising strategies [brainstorm, talk, conference] to clarify ideas during and after writing	■	■	■	■	■	■
Revises selected drafts to improve progression and clarity of ideas	■	■	■	■	■	■
Revises selected drafts to include more descriptive and sensory detail	■	■	■	■	■	■
Uses a variety of reference materials to revise [dictionary, thesaurus, Internet, proofreading checklist]	■	■	■	■	■	
Comments constructively on peers' writing and attempts to use peer comments in a constructive way		■	■	■	■	■

Writing – Sentence Structure and Grammar	K	1	2	3	4	5
Uses basic capitalization and punctuation rules		■	■	■	■	■
Uses complete sentences and recognizes correct word order		■	■	■	■	■
Uses simple and complex sentences			■	■	■	■
Uses singular and plural nouns correctly in writing		■	■	■	■	■
Demonstrates an understanding of subject-verb agreement			■	■	■	■
Uses appropriate parts of speech			■	■	■	■
Identifies subjects and predicates					■	■
Demonstrates understanding of subject and verb agreement					■	■
Identifies synonyms, antonyms, homonyms, homophones, and eponyms					■	■
Demonstrates understanding of proper nouns and proper adjectives					■	■
Identifies and reads abbreviations, initial-letter words, and acronyms					■	■
Identifies and reads blends and clips					■	■

Writing – Penmanship	K	1	2	3	4	5
Writes letters of the alphabet	■	■				
Writes clearly and legibly		■	■	■	■	■
Allows adequate spacing between letters, words, and sentences	■	■	■	■		

Literary Response – Analysis	K	1	2	3	4	5
Distinguishes types of genre		■	■	■	■	■
Distinguishes fantasy from reality	■	■	■	■	■	■
Distinguishes fact from opinion			■	■	■	■
Understands role of author and illustrator		■	■	■		
Identifies author's purpose					■	■

Literary Elements

	K	1	2	3	4	5
Identifies character	■	■	■	■	■	■
Identifies plot, including problem and resolution	■	■	■	■	■	■
Identifies setting	■	■	■	■	■	■
Identifies sequence of events	■	■	■	■		
Identifies story structures: beginning, middle, end	■	■	■	■		
Identifies point of view			■	■	■	■
Identifies tone/mood			■	■	■	■
Identifies theme					■	■

Literary Style and Technique

	K	1	2	3	4	5
Compares and contrasts characters, plots, and settings		■	■	■	■	■
Recognizes descriptive language and imagery:	■	■	■	■	■	■
*Alliteration	■	■	■	■	■	■
*Rhythm and rhyme	■	■	■	■	■	■
*Onomatopoeia			■	■	■	■
Understands use of figurative language:			■	■	■	■
*Metaphor					■	■
*Simile				■	■	■
*Personification			■	■	■	■
Identifies author's style of writing					■	■
Understands use of dialogue	■	■	■	■	■	■
Recognizes use of colloquialism, dialect, idioms, and slang					■	■
Recognizes and understands use of humor:	■	■	■	■	■	■
*Exaggeration and hyperbole			■	■	■	■
Identifies use of foreshadowing and flashbacks				■	■	■
Recognizes use of allusion						■
Recognizes use of suspense					■	■
Identifies use of repetition of language	■	■	■	■	■	■
Identifies use of irony, sarcasm, and satire						■
Recognizes and understands use of symbolism						■

Nonfiction Skills

	K	1	2	3	4	5
Distinguishes nonfiction from fiction	■	■	■	■	■	■
Distinguishes fact from opinion			■	■	■	■
Follows chronological order	■	■	■	■	■	■
Follows steps in a process	■	■	■	■	■	■
Compares and contrasts information	■	■	■	■	■	■
Classifies and categorizes information	■	■	■	■	■	■
Relates cause and effect situations			■	■	■	■
Summarizes what has been read		■	■	■	■	■
Recognizes differing viewpoints in debatable situations			■	■	■	■
Recognizes that valid theories and predictions are based on facts						■

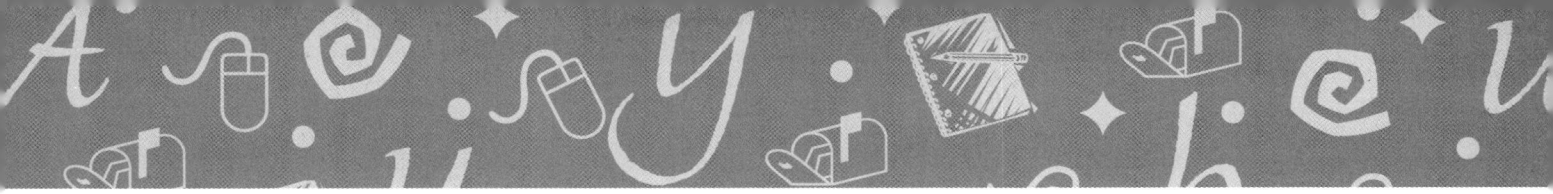

Nonfiction Skills continued	K	1	2	3	4	5
Takes notes on nonfiction reading					■	■
Uses graphic organizers to organize information					■	■

Nonfiction Text Features	K	1	2	3	4	5
Contents	■	■	■	■	■	■
Picture index	■	■	■			
Index		■	■	■	■	■
Glossary		■	■	■	■	■
Labels	■	■	■	■	■	■
Captions	■	■	■	■	■	■
Section headings	■	■	■	■	■	■
Lists / bullet points / inserted information		■	■	■	■	■
Photos and illustrations	■	■	■	■	■	■
Alphabetical order	■	■	■	■	■	■
Sidebars and boxes					■	■

Nonfiction Graphic Elements	K	1	2	3	4	5
Charts	■	■	■	■	■	■
Diagrams		■	■	■	■	■
Scale drawings			■	■	■	■
Time lines	■	■	■	■	■	■
Cutaways / cross sections			■	■	■	■
Maps	■	■	■	■	■	■

Types of Nonfiction	K	1	2	3	4	5
Expository						
*Informative: Description	■	■	■	■	■	■
History					■	■
Interview			■	■	■	■
*Explanatory: Procedural, how-to	■	■	■	■	■	■
Question and answer	■	■	■	■	■	■
Compare and contrast				■	■	■
Cause and effect					■	■
Problem and solution					■	■
Narrative						
Narrative account	■	■	■	■	■	■
Biography			■	■	■	■
Personal profile			■	■	■	■
Journal		■	■	■	■	
Persuasive						
Debate						■
Reference	■	■	■	■	■	■

Mini-lessons for Grade 5

The following pages contain 64 Mini-lessons organized in five sections according to the steps of the writing process. The section titles are: *Prewriting, Drafting, Revising, Publishing,* and *Assessment.* See pages 10 and 11 of this guide for further explanation of these sections.

The Mini-lessons should not be taught strictly in the sequence they appear. You are encouraged to pick and choose lessons from each of the five sections as they are developmentally appropriate for the students in your classroom. For example, you will need to use lessons from the prewriting section throughout the school year to help students find new writing topics and to encourage them to try different formats of writing. You will need to teach elements of drafting, revising, and publishing throughout the year as students work on new pieces. Or you can use the suggested teaching sequence, found on page 198, that links the Mini-lessons to the reading and writing skills and strategies taught in the *Rigby Literacy Comprehension Quarterlies.*

Many of the Grade 5 Mini-lessons include samples of modeling think-alouds, skills, and strategies. You may want to create your own modeling passages based on personal experience using those provided as a springboard for ideas. For further information regarding the teaching of the Mini-lessons, see pages 6–9 of this guide.

Growing as Teachers and Writers . . .

With **Wonder Writers,** you will grow as a more reflective and effective writing teacher while your students grow as writers. The comprehensive and detailed lesson plans ensure that you will be teaching the skills and strategies students need. You will learn about students as individuals and about yourself as a writer as you personalize the lessons with your own writing and modeling. **Wonder Writers** invites you and your young writers to try new strategies and techniques, discover authors, and explore many types of writing and related literature. We hope both you and the students in your class will enjoy discovering the wonder of writing.

What Can I Write? Genre Review: Fiction

Lesson Background

An understanding of the characteristics of different fiction genres will enhance students' reading experiences and broaden the choices they make as they plan their own writing. This mini-lesson helps students develop a better understanding of different genres and provides them with an opportunity to write in a genre of their choice.

Teaching the Lesson

1. Remind students that there are many genres, or categories, of fiction. Ask students to name some types of fiction and list them on the board or on chart paper. Mention that many writers specialize in writing one type of fiction, but that others write in multiple genres. Young writers should experiment with many different genres.

2. Display the chart, noting that its purpose is to compare the characteristics of three different genres of fiction. Then display and briefly summarize three fiction books: one historical fiction, one mystery, and one science fiction/fantasy. (See the You Will Need box for suggested titles.)

3. Ask students, "Which of the three books is historical fiction? How do you know this?" As students discuss the characteristics they used to identify the genre, record their answers in the genre chart. If necessary, use prompts such as, "What is important about the characters in historical fiction?"

4. Repeat the exercise for the remaining books and genres. Use the chart to help students understand the essential characteristics of a genre. For example, point out that in historical fiction, the setting (the time and the place) is especially important; while in a mystery, the characters (detectives, suspects) and other elements (a puzzle, clues) are vital.

5. Invite students to choose a genre and begin planning a story. Have them refer to the chart to be sure that they include all the essential elements of the genre in the story they are planning. Students may use a Story Map (see *Rigby Literacy Graphic Organizer Book,* page 39), a rough outline, or a brief summary to plan their stories.

Practicing the Skill

Have students develop their story plans into rough drafts. Then group students working in the same genre. Students should read their stories aloud to the group, and discuss how each one fits into the genre.

You Will Need

- chart paper
- markers
- three books: one historical fiction, one mystery, and one science fiction/fantasy

Suggested trade titles include:
- *Number the Stars* by Lois Lowry (historical fiction)
- *The Westing Game* by Ellen Raskin (mystery)
- *Indian in the Cupboard* by Lynne Reid Banks (science fiction/fantasy)

- genre chart (below) copied onto chart paper

	Historical Fiction	Mystery	Science Fiction/ Fantasy
Characters			
Setting (time and place)			
Other important elements			

Assessment Connection

As students plan their stories, note their ability to include the essential elements of the genre. Refer to the chart created in class to help students understand where their stories may lack elements of their chosen genre.

What Can I Write? Genre Review: Nonfiction

Lesson Background

Fifth graders are called on more and more to use nonfiction sources to gather information, as well as to write various nonfiction pieces. This mini-lesson helps students develop a better understanding of different nonfiction genres.

Teaching the Lesson

Divide students into small groups. Distribute a selection of nonfiction pieces to each group, and allow time for students to examine the writings. Include biography, autobiography, informational books, how-to books, newspaper articles, and so on.

You've looked at several pieces of writing on many different topics. What do all of these writings have in common? *Help students understand that all of the writings are factual, or nonfiction.* Even though these writings look different—they have different lengths and different formats—they are all nonfiction. As you know, fiction includes many different genres, and nonfiction does, too. Let's identify some of the nonfiction genres we have here. *Ask volunteers to identify the genres of specific books or articles. Discuss the characteristics of each, and record them on chart paper.*

Readers of nonfiction want to be sure that the information they read is accurate. Most times, a nonfiction writer must do research to learn about a topic before beginning to write. Let's brainstorm different ways a writer might research a nonfiction topic. *Record students' responses on chart paper. Their responses may include books, newspaper and magazine articles, reference books, Web sites, interviews, and personal experience.*

Now let's brainstorm some nonfiction topics you might be interested in writing about. *Record students' responses on chart paper.* Which nonfiction genres would be appropriate for each topic? For example, a topic about a person might be expanded into a biography.

Now choose a nonfiction topic that interests you and a genre that would be appropriate for it. Then jot down a few notes on where you might find the information you need to write your piece.

Practicing the Skill

- Provide access to appropriate reference materials for students' research. Have students write short nonfiction pieces based on their research.
- Review correct bibliographic form, and have students write bibliographies for their articles.

Making a Topics List

Lesson Background

Having a topics list can help students make good use of their time and eliminate having "nothing to write about." An ongoing topics list also helps students see story and writing ideas in their daily lives. In this mini-lesson, students learn techniques for identifying writing topics and then create topics lists.

Teaching the Lesson

1. Explain to students that story ideas are everywhere; the trick is to notice them. Draw a web on chart paper and label it "Finding Great Topics to Write About." Show students *Class Clown* (Joanna Hurwitz), *Number the Stars* (Lois Lowry), and *My Life in Dog Years* (Gary Paulsen). Briefly summarize each book and show the cover.

2. Tell students that when Hurwitz was visiting a school, she saw a boy stick his head through the opening in a chair. Wondering what kind of kid would do this and what would happen if he got stuck gave her the idea for the book *Class Clown*. Tell students, "Joanna Hurwitz got a story idea from one small detail. I'll write 'Notice details about people' in our web."

3. From a Danish friend, Lois Lowry learned about the history of Denmark during World War II. Lowry's interest grew, and she began to read more on the subject. The result was her Newbery Award–winning book, *Number the Stars*. Ask the students, "What can we add to our web based on this example?" (Friends can provide topics; reading and research provide topics.)

4. Each chapter in Gary Paulsen's book *My Life in Dog Years* tells an anecdote about one of his dogs. This book follows advice often given to writers: write about what you know. Ask, "What can we add to our web based on this example?" (Draw from your experiences.)

5. Have students make their own topics webs. Ask volunteers to share their ideas and add them to the web on the chart paper.

Practicing the Skill

- Have students make writing topics lists in their writing notebooks. Remind students to use the topics web as a springboard to find story ideas.

- Have students add at least two ideas to their topics list each week.

You Will Need

Suggested trade titles for this lesson include:
- *Class Clown* by Joanna Hurwitz
- *Number the Stars* by Lois Lowry
- *My Life in Dog Years* by Gary Paulsen
- chart paper

Teacher Tip

Authors' autobiographies often show how personal experiences inspire stories. Read aloud *The Moon and I* by Betsy Byars, a delightful and humorous book in which the author reveals the real people and events that inspired many of her novels.

Assessment Connection

Meet with students individually to discuss their topics lists. Ask each student to star two or three topic ideas that most inspire him or her.

Finding/Recording Ideas for a Writer's Notebook

PUBLISHING POWER

Publishing Power

Be sure there are procedures in place that encourage interested students to publish ideas from their writing notebooks—even when they do not represent finished work. For example, students could record poetic phrases and creative ideas from their notebooks on a class chart titled "Inspirations." Other students could then refer to the chart for ideas.

ASSESSMENT

Assessment Connection

If students' notebooks are private, check in periodically with each student to discuss how he or she is using his or her writer's notebook. Encourage students to share a few pages so that you can review the types of things they record. Scheduling regular times to write will ensure that all students use their writer's notebooks regularly.

Lesson Background

A writer's notebook is a powerful tool that can help students think about, respond to, and write about their everyday experiences. In this mini-lesson, students learn how to find writing ideas and how to use a writer's notebook to record those ideas.

Teaching the Lesson

1. Ask students, "Have you ever seen an artist's sketchbook?" Explain that some artists never go anywhere without their sketchbooks, drawing people, places, and things everywhere they go. Later, a sketch may be the inspiration for a painting.

2. Tell students that a writer's notebook is like an artist's sketchbook. It's a place for a writer to record personal feelings or thoughts, interesting experiences, unusual words, snippets of conversation, story ideas, and so on. Display a transparency of BLM 4. Have students read it. Then ask, "What kinds of things did the writer record in her notebook? How might she use the ideas in her notebook?" Allow time for several students to respond.

3. Share the following quotation from Ralph Fletcher's *A Writer's Notebook: Unlocking the Writer Within You:* "Writers are like other people, except for at least one important difference. Other people have daily thoughts and feelings, notice this sky or that smell, but they don't do much about it. All those thoughts, feelings, sensations, and opinions pass through them like the air they breathe. Not writers. Writers react. And writers need a place to record those reactions."

4. Ask students how they might begin a writer's notebook. Encourage them to think of something that happened to them today or something they observed. Did they hear a funny conversation or read a great story? Did something interest them, bother them, or get them wondering? Ask students to think about how they are feeling. Are they proud of something they accomplished? worried? joyous or excited? Encourage them to take time to notice their thoughts, feelings, and experiences and to record them in their writer's notebooks.

Practicing the Skill

Invite students to write in their writer's notebooks whenever inspiration strikes. Reinforce the habit by providing either planned or impromptu "writer's notebook time."

Expanding and/or Connecting Entries in a Writer's Notebook

Lesson Background

Writers use their notebooks as a rich source of ideas and inspiration. This mini-lesson shows students how to revisit their notebooks, looking for entries that can be expanded and/or connected to other ideas to inspire a polished piece of writing.

Teaching the Lesson

1. Tell students that keeping a writer's notebook and writing in it regularly gives a writer a lot of practice in observing and reflecting. However, the benefits don't end there. Explain that periodically, writers go back and reread entries in their notebooks and, as they reread, they look for writing "treasures."

2. On chart paper, make a web and label the center oval "Treasures from a Writer's Notebook." Remind students how you compared a writer's notebook with an artist's sketchbook. Tell them that just as an artist's quick sketch can become the inspiration for a painting, a few lines in a writer's notebook may suggest a great story idea. Draw an oval branching off from the center oval and label it "story idea." Ask students what other "treasures" a writer might discover while rereading his or her notebook. Record students' responses in the web and briefly discuss each one. If necessary, provide prompts to elicit ideas, such as a phrase that inspires a poem, an issue the writer cares greatly about, or a unique character.

3. Point out that the web shows many ways a writer's notebook might provide starting points for a writer to expand an idea, a topic, or even a few well-chosen words into a longer, more polished piece of writing.

4. Have students go back and reread several entries in their writer's notebooks, looking for "treasures" of their own. Remind students that these are their *personal* notebooks, so they can make notes, underline, or circle any entries that interest or excite them. Encourage them to write comments in the margins such as "great character," "good story idea," "nice phrase," and so on. Ask students to find one or two "treasures" that they can use in their next piece of writing.

Practicing the Skill

Have students plan and write a story or poem that draws on an idea, character, or expression from their writer's notebooks. Challenge students to make connections between two entries, or between an older entry and a more recent experience, to use as the basis for a story.

You Will Need

- chart paper
- markers

Teacher Tip

Share with students Ralph Fletcher's image of using a notebook to "incubate a seed," leaving it for a time, and then rereading it later when the time is right to find that the seed has "germinated." (See *A Writer's Notebook: Unlocking the Writer Within You* by Ralph Fletcher, Chapter 11.)

Assessment Connection

Schedule individual conferences with students to review the ways each one uses his or her notebook to get inspiration for writing. Help students see that one word, phrase, or idea in their notebooks can inspire a longer or more developed piece of writing. For reluctant writers, model this process with an idea from your own writer's notebook.

Organizing Ideas for Fiction Writing

You Will Need

- overhead projector
- transparency of a topics list (see Mini-lesson 3)
- transparency of Problems-Solutions Chart BLM (see *Rigby Literacy Graphic Organizer Book*, p. 41)
- transparency of Story Sequence Chart BLM (see *Rigby Literacy Graphic Organizer Book*, p. 11)
- transparency marker
- copies of Problems-Solutions Chart and Story Sequence Chart for each student

Revising Tip

Suggest that students review their graphic organizers during the revising process. They may be reminded of ideas that they want to add or change in their final drafts.

Assessment Connection

Meet with students individually to discuss their completed graphic organizers before they begin writing their stories. Note students who are having difficulty completing their graphic organizers and work with them to organize their story ideas.

Lesson Background

Good story ideas must be developed and organized into a meaningful and logical sequence, including a problem or conflict and a solution. This mini-lesson provides students with tools for developing and organizing their ideas in preparation for story writing.

Teaching the Lesson

1. Display the topics list, and invite students to help you choose a topic for a story.

2. Display the transparency of the Problems-Solutions Chart, and remind students that every story needs to have a problem or conflict. Together, decide on what your story's problem will be, and record it on the chart. Then have students brainstorm and discuss possible solutions, and decide together how to fill in the rest of the chart.

3. Point out that the completed Problems-Solutions Chart will be valuable in writing the story, but that you still must plan the order in which events in the story will happen. Display the transparency of the Story Sequence Chart, and explain that this organizer can provide a "road map" for writing the story. Explain that planning out the major story events in advance will help keep the story focused and on track. Help the class work together to develop ideas for story events and complete the Story Sequence Chart.

4. Distribute a Problems-Solutions Chart and a Story Sequence Chart to each student. Invite students to review their personal topics lists and choose a topic for a story. Then have them begin to organize their ideas by completing the organizers.

Practicing the Skill

- Have students use their completed graphic organizers to write a draft of a story.

- Introduce a Character Traits Web and/or a Story Elements Chart (see *Rigby Literacy Graphic Organizer Book,* pages 31 and 15) and have students use these tools to help organize future stories.

- Divide the class into small groups to discuss how the graphic organizers helped them organize their ideas for writing fiction.

Organizing Ideas for Nonfiction Writing

Lesson Background

Students need to have clear, focused ideas before beginning to write a nonfiction piece. Note taking is an important step in planning and writing nonfiction. This mini-lesson is designed to help students develop good organizational and note-taking skills.

Teaching the Lesson

I'm planning to write a nonfiction article about life aboard a spacecraft. *Display the Web BLM transparency.* First, I'm going to organize my thoughts and write down what aspects of spacecraft life I'd like to write about. *Write "Life Aboard a Spacecraft" in the center box.* What are some topics I might want to include in my article? *Guide students to offer ideas, such as "eating in space" and "how gravity affects people on a spacecraft." Record their ideas on the web.*

Now that I have my topics, I'll have to do some research to gather information. I want to remember the information I find, so I'll have to do some note taking.

Help students understand that effective note taking requires a focus, or purpose, and that it requires careful reading to find information that is important and relevant.

I'm going to read my sources carefully. When I find a fact that's both important and relevant to my article, I'll think about how to put it in my own words. I don't need to write complete sentences. I just want to record the important ideas so I don't forget them when it's time to write my article. *Model how to take an idea from the book and briefly reword it for note taking.*

Distribute a copy of the Web BLM to each student. Choose a nonfiction topic from your topics list. Think about what you want to learn about your topic. First, plan out your ideas on the web. Then, choose a source, such as a book or encyclopedia, to begin researching and taking notes for your article.

Practicing the Skill

- Have students use their notes to write a paragraph for a nonfiction article.

- Encourage students to use a variety of sources of information, including other books, magazines, online resources, and so on. Have them use the information they gather to expand their webs. Then have students create outlines for their articles.

You Will Need

- overhead projector
- transparency marker
- transparency of Web BLM (see *Rigby Literacy Graphic Organizer Book,* p. 29)
- copies of Web BLM for each student
- encyclopedias and/or nonfiction books on a variety of topics

Teacher Tip

Refer to the *Rigby Literacy Graphic Organizer Book* for the following organizers, which students may find helpful for this lesson:
- Venn Diagram, p. 21
- Web, p. 29
- KWL Chart, p. 49
- T-Chart, p. 51

Assessment Connection

Review students' webs before they begin writing. Make sure their ideas are organized and supported through research. You may want to conduct periodic observations of students' note taking, and ask students to reflect on their progress in taking focused notes. For those who need extra support, model how you might take notes from a book or encyclopedia.

Finding Writing Models: Chapter Books

You Will Need

- transparency of BLM 8 (Three Excerpts)
- overhead projector

Teacher Tip

Suggested trade titles for this lesson include:
- *All About Sam* by Lois Lowry
- *Charlotte's Web* by E. B. White
- *Dear Mr. Henshaw* by Beverly Cleary
- *Ella Enchanted* by Gail Carson Levine
- *From the Mixed-Up Files of Mrs. Basil E. Frankweiler* by E. L. Konigsburg
- *Hatchet* by Gary Paulsen
- *The Pinballs* by Betsy Byars
- *Sarah, Plain and Tall* by Patricia MacLachlan

Assessment Connection

Read students' adaptations. How does their writing reflect their author of choice? Note students who are having difficulty finding and using writing models. These students may need more practice comparing and analyzing different authors' styles, and may benefit from small-group instruction and/or discussion of elements such as theme, point of view, voice, and sentence structure.

Lesson Background

Writers love to read, and they often find inspiration in other authors' work. This mini-lesson demonstrates how to use favorite chapter books as literary models.

Teaching the Lesson

1. Share the following quotation with students: "Everyone who writes anything is a borrower, because everything we've ever read comes into play when we write." (Nancie Atwell, *In the Middle: New Understandings About Writing, Reading, and Learning,* Chapter 7)

   Explain that reading provides the inspiration for writing. You can learn a lot about writing by studying the work of favorite authors. But stress to students the difference between "literary borrowing" and plagiarism.

2. Ask students to name a few favorite chapter books. Ask, "What was it about the book that made it a favorite, or kept you thinking about it?" When a book's topic or theme is mentioned, point out that a topic can be "borrowed" as the starting point for a new story.

3. Explain that another way to use a chapter book as a model is to borrow a style. Display the transparency. Tell students that these are three excerpts from chapter books by different authors. Each one describes a character who is in some kind of trouble and is feeling bad. Together, discuss the differences in the style, tone, voice, sentence structure, and word choice in the three texts. Point out that any of these elements can serve as a model for students' next pieces of writing.

4. Ask students to think about chapter books they have enjoyed that might serve as writing models. What aspects of the book would they like to borrow? Have them record their ideas in their writer's notebooks.

Practicing the Skill

- Have students select a book they admire, choose a specific theme or aspect of the author's style, and work on adapting it in a piece of their own writing.

- Encourage students to share their experiences—including successes and difficulties—using chapter books as writing models.

Writing for a Specific Audience: Unknown Audiences

Lesson Background

Good writers keep their audience in mind as they write. Writing to an unknown audience, either to an individual or for publication, requires a somewhat formal style. This mini-lesson clarifies the different expectations and conventions for writing to unknown audiences.

Teaching the Lesson

1. Display the transparency and have students read both samples. Ask them to note similarities between the samples, and discuss the fact that they share a common topic: skateboarding and a skateboard park.

2. Then ask students how the samples differ. Help them recognize that the first sample uses more formal language, is impersonal, and makes a point in an organized, logical way. In contrast, the second sample is much more casual and personal.

3. Explain that each sample is the first paragraph of a letter. Ask students to predict who the intended audience of each letter might be and to explain their reasoning. Help students understand that the more formal style of the first sample is appropriate for a letter to an unknown audience, such as a newspaper editor or a city mayor. The casual style of the second sample is appropriate for a personal, friendly letter to a relative or friend.

4. Remind students that writers must always consider their intended audience and fit their writing to the needs and expectations of their readers. Have students brainstorm a list of situations when they might write to an unknown audience; for example, a newspaper article, a letter to be published in a magazine, and so on.

5. Ask students to look through their writer's notebooks. Have them choose a topic and list ideas they would want to convey in a letter or article intended to be read by an unknown audience.

Practicing the Skill

- Have students draft letters or articles for publication in a school newspaper or to submit to a community newspaper.

- Challenge students to write two paragraphs on the same topic. One paragraph should be written for a specific, known audience (friend, relative, parent, or teacher), and one for an unknown audience (politician or newspaper editor).

You Will Need

- overhead projector
- the following writing samples written on a transparency:

There are a lot of good reasons to build a skateboard park in Oakdale. A skateboard park would be a safe place for students to have fun and get exercise. Also, a park would keep skateboarders away from the sidewalks of the busy downtown area.

Wait till you see my new skateboard! It was my birthday present—Mom and Dad really surprised me this year. I'm on it every chance I get. It's hard to find good places to skateboard, though. I wish they'd build a skateboard park in this town.

Assessment Connection

Read students' letters or articles. Note their ability to write in a style appropriate for an unknown audience (relatively formal, impersonal, and reasoned). For those who need extra support, you may want to review the conventions for writing to unknown audiences. Then go over students' letters with them, sentence by sentence, to analyze the tone and language they used.

Choosing and Narrowing a Topic: Focus

You Will Need

- a photograph of your school
- a photograph of your classroom (with students)

Revising Tip

Whenever students encounter difficulty revising their writing, suggest that they first evaluate whether they have taken on too big a topic. Remind them that the first step in a revision may actually be narrowing down the topic.

Assessment Connection

Schedule prewriting conferences with students to discuss their ideas for narrowing down topics to write about. Then read students' drafts. Did they focus on one specific topic? For students who are having difficulty narrowing down broad topics, model the process with several examples, as you did with the topic "our school" in this mini-lesson.

Lesson Background

In his book *What a Writer Needs,* Ralph Fletcher says, "the bigger the issue, the smaller you write." This mini-lesson is designed to help young writers choose a specific topic and then narrow the focus of the topic.

Teaching the Lesson

Display a photograph of your school. I wonder if our school would be a good topic for a story. So much happens here; I could write about the kindergarten class, our new teachers and students, the cafeteria food, the school play, and lots more. *Through discussion, help students understand that "our school" is a much too large and unfocused topic to write about.* Now I see I need to make my topic smaller—to narrow, or focus it. Instead of trying to include everything about the school, maybe I'll write about our class. *Display a photo of your students in the classroom, and mention several classroom-related topics, such as areas of study, friendships, and so on. Again help students understand that the topic is still too broad.*

Nancie Atwell says, "Like a landscape photographer, a writer is confronted with a huge chunk of scenery; like the photographer, the writer chooses a focus—a section to narrow down and depict with care and grace." *(In the Middle: New Understandings About Writing, Reading, and Learning)* So a photographer or a writer may start with a wide view, or topic, and then choose to "zoom in" on a much narrower part. The small part will be focused, specific, and filled with fine details.

Look around our classroom. Imagine that you have a camera. What small things would you choose to focus on, to photograph, and then write about? Start a list in your writer's notebook.

Practicing the Skill

- Have students revisit a writing draft and focus in on a small, specific part of it to write about.

- Ask students to look at their individual topics lists (see Mini-lesson 3) and work to narrow any topics that are too broad. Remind students to "zoom in," as a photographer would when "confronted with a huge chunk of scenery."

Writing a Rough Draft

Lesson Background

This mini-lesson helps students understand that a rough draft—the important first step in getting ideas down on paper—is a work in progress. A rough draft must undergo many revisions during the writing process, before it becomes a finished piece of writing.

Teaching the Lesson

1. Tell students to listen to these synonyms for the word *rough: coarse, shaggy, uneven, unfinished, crude, ungraceful.* Tell them to remember these synonyms when they are writing a rough draft—a first, rough attempt to get a story down on paper. Explain that as they write a rough draft, they don't need to focus on little things such as spelling or finding the perfect word. Tell them that a rough draft is where you concentrate on getting your ideas down on paper before you forget them.

2. Caution students that a rough draft will need many rereadings and revisions. Tell them that the first time they read a draft, they may change a few words, decide to move a sentence, add a phrase, or divide a long section into paragraphs, but they're not done! Tell them that each time they revisit their draft, they'll notice different things, such as a confusing part, a too brief description, or an unnecessary section that should be cut. Remind them that it's important to let some time pass between rereadings—they will be surprised what they notice when they look at a draft with "fresh" eyes.

3. Display the prepared draft. Tell students that this is the beginning of a rough draft of a story. Ask, "What parts are strong? What parts seem weak and need revising? What might be a good addition?" As students respond, make changes and additions directly on the draft. Use different colored markers as each student responds to simulate multiple rereadings and revisions.

4. Now have students write their own rough drafts. Remind them that as they start writing, their work will be rough—unfinished and bumpy. Tell them that when they go back to reread and revise, they will make their writing polished and graceful.

Practicing the Skill

Have students read over their rough drafts. Encourage them to circle or underline parts that will need revision. Students may benefit from reading their drafts to a partner and discussing possible revisions.

You Will Need

- colored pens or markers
- the following rough draft written on chart paper (leave generous margins and spaces between lines):

"Wait," my sister called. "I'm coming too!" I really didn't mind if she came. I'd packed enough brownies for two, anyway. And so what if Sara was only seven, she was usually fun. And plus I thought I might feel braver if I wasn't alone.

Teacher Tip

Remind students that a rough draft is a work in progress. They can change it again and again until it says what they want it to say.

Assessment Connection

Observe and check with students as they revisit and revise their rough drafts. Their revised drafts should show improvement in the flow of the language, the logical development of ideas, and mechanics. Review revision techniques with students who need support in revising their drafts.

Using the Lead to Set Mood

You Will Need

- books that provide examples of mood-setting leads
- chart paper
- sheets of paper torn in half

Suggested trade titles:
- *The Boy Who Owned the School: A Comedy of Love* by Gary Paulsen
- *Dogs Don't Tell Jokes* by Louis Sachar
- *Child of the Owl* by Laurence Yep

Revising Tip

Ask students to revisit stories they have written. Have them identify the moods of their stories and brainstorm alternative leads that effectively convey those moods.

Assessment Connection

On their current writing projects, ask students to jot down words that describe the moods they are attempting to create. Have them underline words in their leads that were chosen to convey that mood.

Lesson Background

According to author Paul Horgan, the lead is "the seed" from which good stories grow. A good lead captures a reader's attention. A lead can also set the atmosphere or emotional feel of the story—its mood. In this mini-lesson, students learn how to create leads to set a mood.

Teaching the Lesson

1. Remind students that the main purpose of a lead is to get the reader's attention. A good lead also helps to set the mood of a story. Have students discuss moods in books they have read. List the moods they discuss on chart paper.

2. Have students practice developing mood-setting leads, using books as examples. Show a book for which the title and cover art provide a hint to its mood. An example is *The Boy Who Owned the School: A Comedy of Love* by Gary Paulsen. Read aloud the text on the inside jacket flap. Ask students to predict the mood of the book. Then have them brainstorm leads to the book that convey the mood of the cover and jacket text. Write the leads on chart paper. Once you have several leads, ask students to decide which one best sets the mood of the story. Finally, read aloud the opening of the book and have students discuss how the author used the lead to set the mood.

3. Share other books with examples of leads that set moods. Some good choices are *Dogs Don't Tell Jokes* by Louis Sachar and *Child of the Owl* by Laurence Yep.

4. Have students form small groups. Ask each group to choose one of the moods from the brainstormed list. Then, have each group create a setting, main character, and story problem or goal. Tell each student in the group to write a lead for their story. Have group members share their leads and decide which one conveys the mood most effectively. Finally, have group members share their chosen leads with the class.

Practicing the Skill

Share this quote by author Thomas Thompson: "Literally, I probably tear up 200 pieces of paper before I get that first paragraph in shape." (*Shoptalk: Learning to Write with Writers* by Donald M. Murray) Hand out sheets of paper torn in half. At the top of each piece of paper, ask students to write the name of a mood. Then ask them to write as many leads for this mood as they can in ten minutes. Have them share their leads with partners and select the most effective one.

Beginnings: Revealing the End at the Beginning

Lesson Background

After students have had some experience in writing leads, they may wish to experiment with the technique of revealing the ending of a story at the beginning. In this mini-lesson, students explore this unusual but effective technique and learn how writers sustain their readers' interest when the ending is known ahead of time.

Teaching the Lesson

1. Remind students that a good lead "hooks" the reader, sets the mood, and introduces the story's problem or conflict. Immediately there is suspense: the reader wants to know what will happen, how the main character will solve his or her problem, and how the story will end.

2. Explain that an alternative technique is to reveal something about the ending right at the beginning of the story, as E. L. Konigsburg does in *The View from Saturday*. Ask students if they have ever continued to read a book when they knew how it would end. Then ask what might keep a reader reading when the ending of the story is already known.

3. Remind students that all stories need to have conflict, a source of story tension, or suspense. As the main character struggles with a problem, the reader feels the character's tension along with him or her. A story with an ending that is known must still have tension.

   Point out that readers know in the first chapter of *The View From Saturday* that the sixth grade team makes it to the Academic Bowl finals. However, they don't know how the team was chosen, how they worked together, or how they beat such odds to succeed. Wanting to know these things creates enough tension to hold readers' interest to the end.

4. Have students revisit a story draft and experiment with reworking the story to reveal the ending at the beginning. Later, encourage students to discuss the process that this involved.

Practicing the Skill

- In groups, ask students to look for and share examples of stories and books where the ending is revealed in the beginning.

- Have students experiment with revealing the ending at the beginning in a nonfiction essay. For example, an essay could begin with the statement "When the sun rose, the sight of the American flag inspired Francis Scott Key to write a poem that became 'The Star Spangled Banner.'" The essay could then tell the story of the battle that raged over Fort McHenry and how Key came to witness it.

Teacher Tip

Read *Louis the Fish* by Arthur Yorinks. Discuss with students how the author sustains tension throughout the book. Ask students to consider why Yorinks chose to reveal the ending on the first page of the story.

Assessment Connection

Revealing the ending at the beginning is a difficult technique. Read students' revised story drafts. Did they reveal the ending at the beginning? Were they also able to sustain tension or interest throughout the piece? For students who are having difficulty sustaining tension once the ending of a story is known, review ways to maintain the tension in their writing.

Writing Paragraphs: Review

You Will Need

- overhead projector
- transparency marker
- transparencies of BLM 14 and BLM 14A (Writing Paragraphs)

Teacher Tip

You may wish to have students read the sections on paragraph formation and types of paragraphs in the *Writer's Handbook,* pages 38–41.

Publishing Power

Display examples of student writing that show good use of paragraphing conventions on a bulletin board titled "Pleasing Passages."

Assessment Connection

As you evaluate students' writing, note how they organize and use paragraphs in descriptive, narrative, persuasive, and expository writing. Also note their use of paragraphs when writing dialogue. Does the paragraph change each time the speaker changes? Review the conventions of paragraphs with students who need more guidance.

Lesson Background

Clear, disciplined writing requires a thorough understanding of the uses and conventions of paragraphs. Use this mini-lesson to review the rules and purposes of dividing writing into paragraphs.

Teaching the Lesson

1. Remind students that the purpose of writing is to communicate, so writing clearly is an important goal. Explain that one way to make your writing clear is to follow the conventions for dividing text into paragraphs.

2. Display the transparency with no paragraph indents, and ask students to read the text. Then point out that this text is confusing because no paragraphs are indicated. Remind students that each new idea or new speaker requires a separate paragraph.

3. Ask students to suggest ways to separate the displayed writing into paragraphs and to explain their reasons.

4. When students have identified the four paragraphs correctly, display the correct version of the text, and direct students to look at the first paragraph. Explain that in order to present information clearly, each paragraph needs to deal with one topic, which is stated in a topic sentence. The remaining sentences should support the topic and sum up the ideas stated in the paragraph. For each paragraph, ask: "What is the topic sentence of this paragraph? What details support it?"

5. Review with the class the different types of paragraphs and the purpose of each. Guide students to discuss narrative, descriptive, persuasive, and expository paragraphs.

6. Remind students of the editing symbol for a new paragraph. Have students revisit a draft of their writing and check the paragraphing, making corrections as necessary.

Practicing the Skill

- Have students write a story that includes dialogue. Remind them that every new idea should be introduced in a new paragraph. Also, remind them that every time the speaker changes, a new paragraph is necessary.

- Encourage students to examine a few pages of a favorite book, noting how the author divides the text into paragraphs.

Writing with Clarity

Lesson Background

We write to communicate, so it's important to write with clarity to ensure the reader's understanding. In this mini-lesson, students look closely at a writing sample as well as their own writing to learn how to edit for clarity.

Teaching the Lesson

1. Display the first passage on the transparency. Ask students to read it and consider whether the writer has clearly communicated his or her ideas. Have students point out which parts are confusing, and why. For example, the Big Dipper is the most well-known *what?* Does this passage take place in the present or the past? The word *look* in *I look up at the sky* indicates that it is happening in the present, but the word *was* in . . . *amid all of those stars was the Big Dipper* . . . indicates that it happened in the past.

2. Display the second passage on the transparency. Allow students time to read it and compare it to the previous passage. Together, discuss the changes that were made. Encourage students to identify specific changes that make this version clearer. For example:

   - The tense is consistent, so it's clear that the passage takes place in the present.

   - The sentence order is changed to a logical sequence, and the signal words "next" and "when" are added.

   - The unclear pronoun "it" is eliminated in the last sentence.

   - Clearer, more thorough explanations are provided; for example, "I looked for pointer stars at the end" is more fully explained.

   - Incomplete sentences are revised.

   - Punctuation is corrected.

3. Ask students to choose a draft of their writing to evaluate for clarity. Have them revise their drafts to communicate their ideas as clearly as possible.

Practicing the Skill

Pair students after they have revised their drafts. Have pairs read each other's work and ask questions or make suggestions that will help the writer clarify his or her writing.

You Will Need

- transparency of BLM 15 (Writing with Clarity)
- overhead projector

Revising Tip

As part of the revision process, suggest that students make a habit of reading their drafts aloud or having a classmate read them. Point out that this is one way to check that ideas are expressed clearly and completely.

Assessment Connection

Evaluate students' drafts for clarity. Note students' ability to edit their writing to make it clearer. If sections of students' drafts are unclear or confusing, point them out and offer specific examples of what and how to revise for clarity.

Language and Word Choice

You Will Need

- chart paper
- marker
- overhead projector
- the following text written on a transparency:

Last year, my father packed up our things and made me move three hundred miles away.

Just over a year ago, my father plucked me up like a weed and took me and all our belongings (no, that is not true—he did not bring the chestnut tree, the willow, the maple, the hayloft, or the swimming hole, which all belonged to me) and we drove three hundred miles straight north and stopped in front of a house in Euclid, Ohio. (from <u>Walk Two Moons</u> *by Sharon Creech, Chapter 1)*

Assessment Connection

As you evaluate students' writing, note their ability to make thoughtful and deliberate word choices. What words did they replace? Did the new words add more power or feeling? Give students feedback about language, focusing on any experimentation with new words, changes in wording in revised drafts, and other descriptive uses of language.

Lesson Background

Writers love words and take time and care choosing just the right ones to convey meaning and feeling. This mini-lesson raises students' awareness of the power of words as a writer's most important tool.

Teaching the Lesson

When Gary Paulsen was asked, "What is the best part of being a writer?" he replied, "the dance with words" (from *Author Talk,* edited by Leonard S. Marcus). What do you think he meant?

Writers make choices. Which story to tell, what to include, what to leave out, whose point of view to highlight—these are just a few decisions a writer makes each time he or she starts a story. Did you ever think of *words* as choices, too? Good writers choose words with care, trying to create just the right feeling, or to convey a very specific meaning.

Think about how you might describe trees with no leaves. *List responses on chart paper.* Now listen to this writer's description: "In November, the trees are standing all sticks and bones." (from *In November* by Cynthia Rylant)

Why did the writer choose the words "sticks" and "bones"? How does this description make you feel? Do the words make you think about bare trees in a new way? *Encourage discussion.*

Help students to understand that careful, deliberate word choice creates meaningful and powerful writing. Display the transparency and ask students to discuss Creech's choice of words. Why do you think the writer decided to use the word "plucked"? What kinds of things do you usually think of plucking? What feeling does the narrator's description of herself as a "weed" evoke? Why do you think Creech wrote "straight north" instead of just "north"?

Now, revisit a draft of your writing and consider places where words that are more powerful, evocative, or specific might be substituted. Circle words you want to replace.

Practicing the Skill

Have students brainstorm new words to replace the ones they circled in their drafts. Encourage them to use a thesaurus for new word ideas. Then have them add examples of powerful word choices to the classroom Word Wall.

Describing Action and Events: *Showing* Rather Than *Telling*

Lesson Background

This mini-lesson explores the difference between writing that *tells* and writing that *shows*. Effective writers don't tell readers everything; instead, they convey meaning by using descriptive details to illustrate ideas, create settings, and bring characters to life.

Teaching the Lesson

1. Write the following sentences on chart paper:

   My neighbor, Mrs. Elliot, is so nice.

   Every spring, Mrs. Elliot takes us hiking and shows us how to find treasures like violets, snowdrops, and nests of baby birds.

2. Ask students to discuss the difference between the two sentences. You might ask students which sentence encourages the reader to form an opinion, which sentence tells why Mrs. Elliot is nice, and what the most important difference is between the sentences.

3. Explain that the first sentence *tells* the reader that Mrs. Elliot is nice, while the second sentence *shows* that she is nice. The second sentence uses descriptive detail to give a sense of the character. It lets the reader think, form an opinion, and gain meaning.

4. Point out to students that good writers try to *show* more than *tell*. Writers can *show* what a character is like through the use of physical details, spoken words, and actions. Explain that physical details can also bring a setting to life by showing how it looks, feels, sounds, or smells.

5. Pair students. Have each student write a sentence that simply *tells* about a person or place. Then have partners rewrite each other's sentences, replacing the description with dialogue or action. For example, "Gus was angry" can become "Gus slammed his fist against the desk."

Practicing the Skill

- Have students search through books to find examples of details, dialogue, and actions that *show* or illustrate an idea, setting, or character. Have students read their passages aloud. Discuss what the writer *shows* in each passage without stating it directly.

- On index cards, write phrases for ideas, settings, or characters. Distribute the cards, and have students write a paragraph about their topics using descriptive details, dialogue, or actions that *show* rather than *tell* about their topic.

Perspective/Point of View: Changing Point of View

You Will Need

- one copy of BLM 18 (Point of View Chart) for each student
- chart paper

Suggested trade titles:
- *The Three Little Pigs* by Paul Galdone
- *The True Story of the Three Little Pigs by A. Wolf* by Jon Scieszka
- *That Awful Cinderella* by Alvin Granowsky
- *Two Bad Ants* by Chris Van Allsburg

Teacher Tip

The Point of View Chart BLM can be used to compare the characters' points of view in the same book or the characters' points of view in two different story versions.

Assessment Connection

Keep track of students who have difficulty determining point of view and using it in their writing. Give these students additional practice with the concept by having pairs orally retell a story or read a passage from another character's perspective.

Lesson Background

A story can change depending on who is telling it. How an event is perceived can change dramatically if the narrator of the story changes. This mini-lesson illustrates the importance of a character's point of view and helps students understand how changing the point of view from which the story is told affects the story.

Teaching the Lesson

1. Read aloud a traditional version of *The Three Little Pigs,* such as Paul Galdone's book. (If the suggested trade titles are not available, use other appropriate books for this lesson.) After reading, ask, "What do you know about the pigs? What were they like? What do you know about the wolf? What was he like? Who is telling the story?" Record students' responses on chart paper.

2. Explain that all writing has a perspective, or point of view. Each person's point of view, or way of looking at and experiencing events, is unique. Two friends arguing—or even enjoying an activity together—have different points of view. Explain that the world looks different depending upon who we are. Read aloud *The True Story of the Three Little Pigs by A. Wolf.* Repeat the questions about the characters and the storyteller and again record students' responses.

3. Have students look at a specific event or character that appears in each book, such as the wolf. Using the responses on the chart as a guide, have students contrast how the wolf is viewed in the traditional tale with his portrayal in the second story. Then have students complete the Point of View Chart BLM. Ask students, "How does changing the point of view change the story?"

4. If possible, read aloud one of Alvin Granowsky's rewritten fairy tales, such as *That Awful Cinderella.* His books tell fairy tales from two different perspectives. Have students discuss the different points of view.

Practicing the Skill

- Have students rewrite a familiar story from another character's point of view. For example, rewrite *Jack and the Beanstalk* from the giant's perspective.

- Remind students that readers "see" and hear the narrator's point of view, so it is important to be aware of who is telling the story. Have students revisit books they have previously read and identify the character from whose point of view the story is told.

Developing a Character Through Thoughts, Feelings, and Actions

Lesson Background

A character's thoughts, feelings, and actions reveal his or her personality. This mini-lesson shows students how characters can be developed by including what Nancie Atwell calls "all that interior stuff—reflections, dreams, thoughts, and feelings . . . " (*In the Middle: New Understandings About Writing, Reading, and Learning,* Chapter 6).

Teaching the Lesson

1. Remind students that characters are a key element in any story. Explain that authors develop characters by revealing their thoughts, feelings, and actions. Display the Character Chart as shown below on chart paper.

Character Chart

Book Title: _____

Character's Name: _____

Thoughts, Feelings, Actions	What This Shows About the Character

2. Read aloud the passage from *Ramona the Pest* by Beverly Cleary that begins, "Ramona was filled with the glory . . ." found in Chapter 7 and the passages from *My Side of the Mountain* by Jean Craighead George that begins, "Wonder filled me as I realized . . ." and end, ". . . a harassing but wonderful friendship" found in Chapter 9.

3. Have students choose one character and identify the character's thoughts, feelings, and actions. Record students' responses on the chart. Then ask them to make inferences about the character based on the character's thoughts, feelings, and actions, and record these as well.

4. Ask students to choose a character from one of the passages you read and list adjectives that describe him or her. Refer students back to the passage to find the specific thoughts, feelings, and actions of the character that support their descriptions.

Practicing the Skill

Have students write about a character of their choice, focusing on his or her thoughts, feelings, or actions.

You Will Need

- Character Chart written on chart paper (see Teaching the Lesson)
- fiction books that students have recently read

Suggested trade titles:
- *Ramona the Pest* by Beverly Cleary
- *My Side of the Mountain* by Jean Craighead George

Teacher Tip

If you cannot locate the books that are suggested for this lesson, use others that model the same concepts.

Assessment Connection

Note which students need extra support and practice in using thoughts, feelings, and actions to develop or describe a character. Pair these students and ask each one to write a description of the same character. Then have partners compare their descriptions.

Writing Dialogue

You Will Need

- chart paper
- writing samples A and B (below) written on chart paper

Suggested trade title:
Charlotte's Web by E. B. White

Sample A
Fern begged her father not to kill the pig.

Sample B
"Please don't kill it!" she sobbed. "It's unfair."

Mr. Arable stopped walking.

"Fern," he said gently, "you will have to learn to control yourself."

"Control myself?" yelled Fern. "This is a matter of life and death, and you talk about <u>controlling</u> *myself?"*
(<u>Charlotte's Web</u>, Chapter 1)

Assessment Connection

Have students revise a piece of writing to include dialogue. Then have them check and correct punctuation and paragraphing. Ask them to make their revisions in red so that you can see what they've changed. Do their identification tags help the dialogue flow? Is it clear who is speaking? For students who need extra practice with correct paragraphing and punctuation, have them refer to passages in their favorite books as models.

Lesson Background

Well-written dialogue can give readers information about a plot, reveal important details about characters, and move a story forward in a believable and dramatic way. In this mini-lesson, students practice writing dialogue that reveals important information to readers.

Teaching the Lesson

1. Explain that dialogue, or "written talk," is an important part of most good fiction. Display the two samples from *Charlotte's Web* and have students compare and discuss them. Explain that Sample B shows us Fern's feelings through dialogue, while Sample A allows us to infer her feelings in a broad and general way.

2. Remind students that dialogue is a good way of helping the reader form visual images of characters or events. Explain that dialogue can reveal the setting in a story, what and why something is happening, what a character is like, and why he or she feels a certain way.

3. Explain that "identification tags" *(he said, yelled Fern)* tell readers who is speaking. Have students brainstorm words that can replace *said* and list them on chart paper.

4. Point out that identification tags are not always necessary. For example, if only two characters are present, the new paragraph that signals the new speaker may be enough to let readers know who is speaking. Encourage students to practice writing dialogue without identification tags in portions of their own writing where only two characters are talking.

5. Explain that identification tags can be placed in the beginning, at the end, or in the middle of a sentence. Varying the placement of tags makes the writing more interesting.

6. Pair students. Have each student write a short summary of a scene from a book involving two people. Then have partners rewrite each other's scenes using dialogue. Remind students that dialogue should sound like natural speech.

Practicing the Skill

- Have students listen to a conversation and write it as dialogue.

- Have students write a scene in two ways: as a narrative summary and as a dramatic scene including dialogue. Encourage students to use dialogue to show important information about the characters, action, and setting of a story.

Developing Background Information

Lesson Background

Stories need more than a bare-bones plot to give readers a sense of settings, situations, and characters. Writers need to include background information to engage readers and help them fully understand a story. This mini-lesson helps students "read between the lines" to discover the background information writers provide.

Teaching the Lesson

Have you ever told a story and found that your listeners had questions or were confused? If so, you probably left out some important background information. Perhaps you thought it was information your listeners already knew; perhaps you forgot an important detail. Either way, your listeners couldn't fully enjoy or even understand the story because important information was missing.

Background information is important, whether a story is spoken or written. *Choose a story the class has read.* What background information did the author provide in this story? *List students' answers on chart paper. Responses may include events that happened before the story began; characters' ages, interests, or hopes; weather or environment; or facts about a historical event or person.* How did the author tell the background information? Sometimes information is stated directly, but other times it is not and the reader has to make inferences to figure out the background information.

Often a writer can use his or her imagination to create background information. At other times, a writer needs to research facts for a story's background. Introduce *The Cabin Faced West,* the story of a young girl experiencing the hardships of pioneer life. If possible, read aloud the passage that begins, "Ann fell silent . . ." found in Chapter 1, and ask students to notice the background information the author provides. If the suggested trade title is not available, use other appropriate books for this lesson.

Have student pairs discuss and record the background information in the passage and its importance to the story.

Practicing the Skill

As students plan a story, have them list background information their readers will need.

You Will Need

- chart paper
- a short story familiar to the class

Suggested trade title:
The Cabin Faced West by Jean Fritz

Assessment Connection

Have students choose a piece of finished or unfinished writing. During individual conferences, ask students to explain what background information they included and why. Do they think their readers will be confused about anything? What can be added to make the writing clearer? For those who need extra support, review together a passage from a familiar story that provides a lot of background information. Ask students to list the type of information the author provided. Have students use the list as a guide to the kinds of background information they can include in their writing.

Developing Plot

You Will Need

chart paper

Suggested trade title:
Bunnicula: A Rabbit-Tale of Mystery by Deborah and James Howe

Assessment Connection

During individual conferences, ask students to share a finished piece of writing and discuss the plot. Are the problem and solution clear to the reader? Do the story events unfold in a logical way? For students who need extra support, suggest that they complete a detailed story map and review it with you before they begin writing.

Lesson Background

The plot, or series of events, is a vitally important element in a story; it is what keeps readers interested. A good plot is what causes readers to say, "I wonder what will happen next!" This mini-lesson helps students understand and plan their own story plots.

Teaching the Lesson

1. Explain to students that plot is an essential element of any story. Elicit from students a definition of plot (the events that happen in a story, including a problem and resolution). Make sure that students understand that plot consists of more than a series of episodes; it must include some kind of problem, conflict, or tension.

2. Ask students to identify the problem or conflict in several stories they have recently read. Then ask how the problems are solved. Lead students to the understanding that in each case, the problem of the story must be solved by the story characters.

3. Together, create a story map based on the plot of a familiar story, such as *Little Red Riding Hood*. On chart paper, write the story's events, a problem from the story, and the solution for that problem.

4. Display and introduce *Bunnicula* or use another appropriate trade title. Explain how the authors work when they write. Tell students that when Deborah and James Howe write, they use an idea from their writer's notebooks, and ask themselves *What if?* questions: *What if the rabbit attacks the vegetables instead of people? What if the girl is painfully shy? What if she's shy because she's afraid of something? What might she be afraid of?* (*Author Talk,* Section 6)

5. Have students work in pairs to make a blank story map and use it to develop a plot. Encourage students to start by thinking of a situation or character and then asking themselves questions about it, as Deborah and James Howe do.

Practicing the Skill

- Have students record plot ideas in their writer's notebooks. Suggest that they include problem and solution ideas and several *What if?* questions to help them expand and develop their ideas.

- Some students may prefer making a rough plot outline as an alternative to making a story map. Have students experiment with both planning techniques.

Making Transitions: Time, Setting, and Point of View

Lesson Background

This mini-lesson introduces an important part of the writers' craft: the use of transitions between different times, settings, and points of view. The use of effective transitions allows writing to flow in a way that helps readers better understand and enjoy the story line.

Teaching the Lesson

1. Discuss with students the meaning of transition: a passage or movement from one state, subject, or place to another. Explain that writers provide transitions to show that time has passed, the action has moved to a different setting, or the point of view has changed to that of a different character. Without transitions, writing can seem choppy or confusing.

2. Explain to students that transitions are needed between scenes or chapters, and that there are several ways to signal these transitions to the reader. Tell students that their choice of words can signal a new time or setting. A paragraph can also lead into a new scene. Explain that a sentence that ends one scene can connect in some way to a sentence that begins a new scene with a different setting, time, or point of view. For example, in *Grindle,* the author ends Chapter 3 with the following:

> Nick barely heard the assignment. His heart was pounding, and he felt small, very small. He could feel the tops of his ears glowing red. A complete shutdown. An extra assignment. And probably a little black mark next to his name on the seating chart.
>
> Everything he had heard about this was true—don't mess around with The Lone Granger.

He then begins Chapter 4 with:

> It was a beautiful September afternoon, bright sun, cool breeze, blue sky. But not for Nick.
>
> Nick had to do a little report for the next day.

Ask students what has changed as Chapter 4 begins (the time and the place). Ask what remains the same and connects the two scenes. (Nick remains upset about the report.)

Practicing the Skill

Have students revisit a story they have previously written. Tell them to look for places in the story where they can use transitions of time, setting, or point of view to improve their writing.

You Will Need

Suggested trade title:
Grindle by Andrew Clements

Teacher Tip

Here are some books with shifting points of view for students to examine:
- *The View from Saturday* by E. L. Konigsburg
- *The Wanderer* by Sharon Creech
- *Bull Run* by Paul Fleischman

Assessment Connection

Note students' ability to identify different types of transitions and use them in their own writing. Can students identify which elements change and which elements provide a connection for readers by remaining the same? Work with students who are struggling with this concept by pointing out examples of effective transitions in familiar books. Have students refer to these passages as models for their own writing.

Putting Voice into Writing

You Will Need

Suggested trade titles:
- *When I Was Young in the Mountains* by Cynthia Rylant
- *Gila Monsters Meet You at the Airport* by Marjorie Weinman Sharmat
- *In November* by Cynthia Rylant
- several copies of biographies written by Jean Fritz

Teacher Tip

Here are some good examples of books that reveal voice:
- *Out of the Dust* by Karen Hesse
- *Journey* by Patricia MacLachlan
- *Our Only May Amelia* by Jennifer Holm

Assessment Connection

As students write in different genres, note their ability to express themselves through the use of voice. Have students who are having difficulty incorporating voice tape-record themselves telling a story from their own experience. Suggest that they listen for expressions or a use of language that is unique to them. Encourage them to write the same story, adding the details that make their voice unique.

Lesson Background

Effective writing has a voice—a use of language that is unique to the writer. The writer's voice makes a piece of writing sound natural and believable, personal and lively. This mini-lesson helps students begin to incorporate their unique personalities, or voice, in their writing.

Teaching the Lesson

1. Ask students, "If you overheard two classmates talking, would you recognize the speakers, even without seeing them?" Discuss qualities that would reveal the speakers' identities: the sound of their voices, the words and expressions they used, the ideas they expressed, and so on. Explain to students that these are the qualities of "voice." Explain that writers can put voice into their writing, and that voice makes their writing personal and unique, lively and powerful.

2. Read aloud from *When I Was Young in the Mountains* or another book in which the author's voice is evident. Explain that Rylant's book tells a personal family story. Discuss with students how the author goes beyond a mere telling of events. What unique expressions does she use? What does the author reveal about personal feelings as she reflects on her childhood experiences?

3. Point out that voice can also bring life to other kinds of writing. Read aloud from *Gila Monsters Meet You at the Airport* by Marjorie Weinman Sharmat, and discuss how the author uses voice to reveal the character and inner life of this fiction story's narrator.

4. Explain that a writer's personality and voice can come through even in nonfiction writing. Read aloud from *In November* by Cynthia Rylant, and have students discuss how this book differs from many conventional nonfiction books about seasonal change.

5. Divide students into small groups. Provide each group with one of Jean Fritz's biographies and an encyclopedia passage on the biography's subject. Have students read the passage and the first chapter of the biography and then compare the two. Discuss with students Fritz's use of voice in her nonfiction writing.

Practicing the Skill

Have students write or revise a piece of writing with particular attention to voice. Encourage them to read their writing aloud, either to themselves or to a partner, to hear what sounds natural and personal in their writing, and what sounds awkward or contrived.

Endings: Circular Endings

Lesson Background

One way to bring a story to a satisfying and clever conclusion is through a circular ending. A circular ending occurs when a story ends where it began. This mini-lesson helps students identify, analyze, and write their own circular endings.

Teaching the Lesson

1. Read aloud *If You Give a Mouse a Cookie* or use another appropriate trade title. Ask students what they notice about the ending of the story. (The story ends where it begins.) Explain that this is an example of a circular ending. The story has come full circle; the end connects with the beginning. A circular ending gives a story balance and is satisfying to readers.

2. Point out that adventure and fantasy stories often have circular endings. The story often begins with the main character, or hero, at home. The hero sets out on an adventure or quest, encounters danger, triumphs over it, and then returns home. Stress that while the ending connects with the beginning, it is not exactly the same. Often, the difference is that the character has learned something important or changed in some way. Have students discuss a familiar story, such as *The Wizard of Oz* by L. Frank Baum, and decide whether it has a circular ending, and why.

3. Explain that a circular ending can be achieved in different ways. A story can start and end at the same place, such as home. Or it can begin and end with a similar situation, mood, or a piece of dialogue that refers back to something said in the beginning of the story.

4. Have students work in groups to discuss stories they have previously read and books that have circular endings. What makes each ending circular? Has the main character or any other element changed? In what way?

Practicing the Skill

- Have students work in pairs to plan their own circular story. Tell them to make a story map to plan the events, conflict, and resolution in their stories. Encourage pairs to begin writing a rough draft when they are ready.

- Have students write their own story with a circular ending.

You Will Need

Suggested trade title:
If You Give a Mouse a Cookie by Laura Numeroff

Teacher Tip

Books featuring circular endings:

Picture books
- *The Polar Express* by Chris Van Allsburg
- *Where the Wild Things Are* by Maurice Sendak

Chapter books
- *Holes* by Louis Sachar
- *Matilda* by Roald Dahl
- *The Phantom Tollbooth* by Norton Juster

Assessment Connection

Note students' ability to identify and analyze circular endings, as well as to plan and write an original story with a circular ending. Check to see that students' stories end similarly to the way in which they begin. For those students who are having difficulty, help them map out an existing story with a circular ending. Then have students use that map as a model for their own story.

Sentence Structure: Variety

Lesson Background

Correct sentence structure is important in good writing. Varying sentence structure is equally important since it helps to keep the reader's attention. This mini-lesson is designed to help students discover different ways to add variety and interest to their sentences.

Teaching the Lesson

1. Review with students the basics of sentence structure: A sentence consists of a subject and a verb and must contain at least one complete thought. The subject and the verb of a sentence must agree.

2. Write the following sentences on chart paper. Have students identify the subject and verb in each sentence. Discuss how the writer has varied the structure in each sentence.

   I watched the deer from my window.
   (prepositional phrase at end of sentence)

   From my window, I watched the deer.
   (prepositional phrase at beginning of sentence)

   The deer looked happy as she licked the salt block.
   (dependent clause at end of sentence)

   As she licked the salt block, the deer looked happy.
   (dependent clause at beginning of sentence)

   The deer was light brown. The deer had a white tail.
   (two simple sentences about how the deer looked)

   The deer was light brown and had a white tail.
   (combining sentences with ideas that go together)

3. Discuss the importance of varying sentence structure. Explain that writing becomes boring if writers write every sentence the same way.

4. Write the following paragraph on chart paper, and have students work in pairs to rewrite it correctly using varied sentence structure. Ask volunteers to read their paragraphs aloud for the class to discuss.

   Raptors were small dinosaurs. Some raptors were only six feet tall. They had sharp teeth. They had hooked claws. They had good eyesight. They could see far. Their eyes pointed forward.

Practicing the Skill

Have students write a paragraph on a topic of their choice, focusing on using correct and varied sentence structure.

You Will Need

- chart paper
- examples of paragraphs with varied sentence structure

Teacher Tip

- Refer to the "Sentences" chapter beginning on page 34 of the *Writer's Handbook* for more information on subjects, predicates, and types of sentences.
- Mention to students that they may also learn how to vary their sentence structure by imitating sentences written by professional writers.

Assessment Connection

Use anecdotal records, writing samples, and/or a writing checklist to record students' progress in writing correct and varied sentences. For students having difficulty in this area, suggest that they choose a book written for younger students. These books often have very basic sentence structures. Students can practice rewriting these sentences so they are more varied and complex.

Writing a Five-Paragraph Essay: Review

Lesson Background

The five-paragraph essay is a useful and important writing form for students to master. This mini-lesson helps students develop proficiency in planning, organizing, and writing a five-paragraph essay.

Teaching the Lesson

1. Review with students the structure of a five-paragraph essay. Explain that following this format helps writers plan and organize their thoughts for writing. Display a transparency of the Five-Paragraph Essay Format BLM. Tell students that the first paragraph introduces the main idea of the essay and must contain a clear topic sentence. A topic sentence tells the main idea or purpose of the essay.

2. Write a sample topic sentence for a persuasive essay on the board.

   Wilderness camping is a great way to spend a vacation.

   Have students identify the topic of the sentence (wilderness camping as a vacation activity).

3. Explain that the introductory paragraph also contains three subtopic sentences that help support the main idea in the topic sentence. Examples of subtopic sentences are:

   Wilderness camping is a way to see wildlife.

   Camping forces you to be self-reliant.

   Wilderness camping can be relaxing and restful.

4. Explain that the next three paragraphs are the body of the essay. Each paragraph restates one of the three subtopics from the first paragraph. The subtopic becomes the topic sentence of the paragraph. Each subtopic must be supported by three supporting details. Model writing supporting detail sentences, and work with students to write others.

5. Tell students that the concluding paragraph restates the topic of the essay and the three supporting subtopics.

6. Have students choose a topic for a five-paragraph essay and then together complete the Five-Paragraph Essay Format BLM.

Practicing the Skill

- Have students use the completed BLM as a guide to writing a five-paragraph essay.

- Have students practice writing several topic sentences that could be developed into five-paragraph essays.

You Will Need

- overhead transparency of BLM 27 (Five-Paragraph Essay Format)
- overhead projector

Teacher Tip

Explain to students that they should use transition words at the beginning of paragraphs to help readers understand the order of their ideas. Paragraph two can start with *First,* paragraph three then begins with *Second,* and paragraph four starts with *Third.* The fifth paragraph is the summary of the essay and can begin with *In summary* or *In conclusion.*

Assessment Connection

As you read students' essays, check that each begins with a topic sentence followed by three subtopics in the introductory paragraph, has three paragraphs supporting the subtopics, and has a concluding paragraph that restates the topic. For students having difficulty organizing their thoughts, work individually or in small groups to help them complete BLM 27.

Writing Descriptive Text: People Profiles

You Will Need

- chart paper
- books about entertainers, athletes, politicians, health care workers, activists, etc.

Teacher Tip

LITERATURE

Read and discuss several biographical sketches in books similar to these titles:

- *Lives of Extraordinary Women: Rulers, Rebels (And What the Neighbors Thought)* by Kathleen Krull
- *Revolutionary Poet: A Story About Phyllis Wheatley* by Maryann N. Weidt and Mary O'Keefe Young

Assessment Connection

ASSESSMENT

Check students' progress as they work on their people profiles. Did they organize their ideas in a web first? Did they include the most important or most interesting information about the person? Did they check the facts they discovered? If some students are having difficulty, help them brainstorm and organize ideas into a web. Model for them how to work from their web as they write.

Lesson Background

Reading about people is one way to get to know them. Writing about people is another way to get to know them. This mini-lesson helps students learn how to organize and write "people profiles," or biographical sketches.

Teaching the Lesson

1. Ask students to think about what kind of information helps them get to know and understand another person. Write students' responses on chart paper. These may include facts about the person's life, his or her physical appearance, feelings, words, actions, and so on.

2. Explain that a written profile, or *biographical sketch,* includes the same kind of information. Its purpose is to help the reader get to know the subject of the profile. On chart paper, draw an oval and write "People Profile" in the center. Create a web by drawing five spokes radiating from the oval. Draw ovals at the end of each spoke, and label them *facts, description, words, actions,* and *thoughts and feelings.*

3. Have the class choose a well-known person to profile. Ask students to brainstorm ideas about the person for each of the five categories in the web. Guide students by asking questions such as, "What facts are important in understanding _____'s life? Does a reader need to know what country this person was born in or what kind of work he or she does? Has this person done something he or she is famous for, or something especially generous or brave? Can we include the person's words—a quotation—that really shows something important about him or her?"

4. When the web is complete, discuss with students which ideas in the web should be included in a brief, written profile of the subject. Remind students that a "people profile" is descriptive writing; its main purpose is to inform, but it may also entertain.

5. Have students use selected ideas from the web to write a people profile.

ON YOUR OWN

Practicing the Skill

- Have students write a profile of someone they know.

- Have students write a profile of a person they will need to research. Suggest historical figures or people currently in the news as subjects.

Writing Descriptive Text: Advertisements

Lesson Background

Writers of advertising copy choose words carefully and with a specific purpose: to sell a product. This mini-lesson is designed to help students analyze written advertisements and learn how they are written.

Teaching the Lesson

1. Explain that there are different types of writing for different purposes and for different audiences. Have students listen as you read an advertisement from a newspaper or magazine. Ask what the purpose of this writing is and who the target audience is.

2. Point out that people who write advertisements must grab a reader's attention, make a point quickly, and use few words and little space. Explain that advertising is expensive, and that additional space costs more money. Therefore, advertisers choose words carefully.

3. Elicit from students the different purposes of writing: to entertain, to inform, and to persuade. Have students discuss which of these three purposes is relevant to advertising copy. Lead students to an understanding that advertisements are written mainly to persuade, but that the most effective advertisements also inform and even entertain.

4. Divide students into groups to analyze and discuss several advertisements. On chart paper, write prompts such as: *Who is the intended audience? Which words grab your attention? Which words hold your interest and keep you reading? What kind of information about the product is presented? Has the writer attempted to persuade, inform, and/or entertain? Which words were chosen to entertain?* Then have student groups share their analyses with the rest of the class.

5. Have students choose a product and an intended audience and write a short advertisement. Impose a word count to mimic the requirements of real advertisements. Students' writing should attempt to persuade and inform, but they may choose to entertain as well. Remind students to use concise, vivid language in their ads.

Practicing the Skill

- Ask students to find and bring in well-written advertisements. What makes the ad effective? Discuss the writer's word choices.

- Have students write advertisements for the school library, lunch program, after-school activities, or other school services or programs. Let students post their advertisements around the school or publish them in the school newsletter.

You Will Need

- chart paper
- several advertisements from newspapers and magazines

Assessment Connection

Plan individual conferences to review students' advertisements. Is their language direct and vivid? Do the advertisements persuade, inform, and/or entertain? Note students who are having difficulty writing an advertisement to persuade and inform. These students may benefit from organizing their ideas into a web before beginning writing.

Writing Descriptive Text: Reviews of Books, Movies, Television Shows

You Will Need

- chart paper
- several books with blurbs
- a few videos with blurbs
- reviews of books, movies, and TV shows

Assessment Connection

As you read students' reviews, check for the following:
- Has the student stated his or her opinion about the book, movie, or TV show?
- Has the student supported his or her opinion with examples?
- Has the student described the book or movie without giving away the ending?

Publishing Power

Encourage students to publish final, polished book reviews online on a site such as http://www.worldreading.org. (Be sure to remind students that for safety reasons, they should never use their last names online.) Students will also enjoy reading and comparing reviews of favorite books on this site and others like it. Students can also collect their reviews and publish them in a book for next year's class.

Lesson Background

Reviews of books, movies, TV shows, plays, and music fall into a unique category of descriptive writing. This mini-lesson focuses on the techniques of writing informative, descriptive reviews.

Teaching the Lesson

1. Read aloud brief reviews and blurbs about several books, a movie, and a TV show. Ask students to discuss common elements in the reviews, and list their ideas on chart paper. Students' responses may include the following: a review is brief and to the point; it contains an opinion; it describes the book or movie but does not give away the ending; it tells something about the characters; and so on.

2. Discuss with students the purposes of reviews and blurbs: to get people interested in a book or video; to make people want to read a book or view a video; to sell a book or video; and to persuade people that the book or video is good (or poor, if it's an unfavorable review).

3. Ask students to think about how they might persuade a friend to read a book they enjoyed. What kinds of things might they tell their friend? List students' ideas on chart paper. For example, they might: tell one funny incident from the book; tell about the plot without revealing the ending; describe the main problem or conflict; tell about an interesting character; describe an unusual setting; or name other good books the author has written.

4. Remind students that review-writing is a kind of persuasive writing, and that their opinions must be supported with examples. It's not enough to say, "It's a great story!" A reviewer must tell *why* he or she believes a book is great: the suspense is exciting; the main character is always getting into funny situations; and so on.

5. Have students write a book or movie review in which they try to "sell" the book or movie to others. Remind students not to reveal the ending, and to leave their readers with a question or something to anticipate so they'll want to experience the book or movie for themselves.

Practicing the Skill

- Have students search for and bring in examples of well-written, informative, and persuasive reviews to share and analyze.

- Have students write blurbs for classroom or library books.

Writing Narrative Text: Personal Memoirs

Lesson Background

Writers keep journals to record their thoughts and feelings and to practice their writing. Many writers also use their journals as the basis for writing narratives that tell about their personal experiences. This mini-lesson helps students become familiar with writing about their own personal experiences.

Teaching the Lesson

Most successful writers give the same advice: write every day, and write about what you know. One way writers do this is by keeping a journal to record their thoughts, ideas, and experiences. Later, a writer might use an interesting experience from his or her journal to write a longer piece of writing.

Writers often use experiences recorded in their journals to write personal memoirs. A memoir is a narrative that tells about an experience, expresses personal thoughts and feelings, and is meant to be read by an audience. A memoir, like an autobiography, is told from the first-person point of view, or the "I" voice.

If possible, read aloud the short memoir that Cynthia Rylant wrote about her childhood in Appalachia, When I Was Young in the Mountains, *or use another appropriate autobiography. Then ask questions such as:* What facts does this memoir tell you about the author's childhood? What feelings does the author express?

Read aloud excerpts from other autobiographies, such as Jerry Spinelli's Knots in My Yo-Yo String: The Autobiography of a Kid. *Have students discuss the feelings the author presented in his or her writing and what character traits were evident from reading the passage.*

Many memoirs relate experiences that might seem ordinary. Their significance comes from the writers' strong feelings about their experiences. Choose an experience that you feel strongly about and begin to write your own memoir.

Practicing the Skill

- Have students read a memoir and discuss how the writer expresses personal thoughts and feelings about the experiences he or she describes.
- Have students write a short memoir based on an entry in their writer's notebooks.

You Will Need

Suggested trade titles:
- *When I Was Young in the Mountains* by Cynthia Rylant
- *Knots in My Yo-Yo String: The Autobiography of a Kid* by Jerry Spinelli

Teacher Tip

Read aloud excerpts from authors' autobiographies. Here are some possible titles.
- *Bill Peet: An Autobiography* by Bill Peet
- *Boy: Tales of Childhood* by Roald Dahl
- *Homesick: My Own Story* by Jean Fritz

Assessment Connection

Read each student's personal memoir. Did the student convey strong feelings about his or her experiences? For those students having difficulty writing their memoirs, have them tell you about a real-life experience they feel strongly about. Students may find that talking about ideas first makes it easier for them to put their ideas into writing.

Writing Narrative Text: Chapter Books

You Will Need

- chart paper
- a selection of chapter books

Suggested trade title:
Holes by Louis Sachar

Teacher Tip

- Good transitions between chapters help to weave a chapter book together. Provide students with examples of suspenseful chapter endings such as the following:
"Then a dark hand and an orange sleeve reached up out of the tunnel." (*Holes*, Chapter 34)
- See Mini-lesson 23, Making Transitions, for more help.

Assessment Connection

Review students' story maps with them. Do their plans include characters, setting, problem, and solution? Do their plans make sense? For students who need extra support, help them create a story map of a chapter book they have already read. Reversing the process may make it easier for them to see how all the story elements fit together.

Lesson Background

Writing longer narratives such as chapter books requires careful planning. This mini-lesson is designed to help students make the leap from writing short stories to writing longer fiction pieces.

Teaching the Lesson

Writers do a lot of planning when they write chapter books. Just as artists make sketches before starting a painting, writers make story maps and notes about characters before starting a chapter book. To plan a chapter book, first decide who the story will be about (characters) and what problem the main character will face (conflict). *On chart paper, draw a blank story map that includes the headings* Main Character, Problem, Attempts to Solve the Problem, *and* Solution. *Have students brainstorm ideas about a main character and a conflict he or she might face.*

Think of your chapter book in three sections: beginning, middle, and end. You will divide these three parts into chapters later on.

- The beginning of a story introduces the characters and the setting, gives background information, and indicates what kind of story this will be, such as mystery, fantasy, science fiction, and so on. The problem is introduced here, too.
- In the middle, the longest section, the characters do different things to try to solve the problem. Newbery Medalist Marion Dane Bauer makes this suggestion for beginning fiction writers: "Have the main character make three attempts to solve the problem. Build tension by having the easiest attempt first and the hardest, or most important, last." (*What's Your Story? A Young Person's Guide to Writing Fiction,* Chapter 6)
- The end of your book should be short; its purpose is to tie up loose ends so the reader is satisfied.

Let's look at our story map. How will our character try to solve his or her problem? How will he or she actually solve it? *Complete the story map together.*

After writing a rough draft, divide your story into chapters. You can create a chapter for each episode or for each attempt to solve the problem. Or you might decide to end each chapter at a suspenseful moment to keep your readers interested. *Have student pairs look at and discuss the chapter divisions in several chapter books.*

Practicing the Skill

Have students create a story map to plan a chapter book.

Writing Narrative Text: Biographies

Lesson Background

Writers often learn about historical figures by researching and writing about them. This mini-lesson increases students' understanding and appreciation of biographies, including how a writer might choose and research a person to be the subject of a biography.

Teaching the Lesson

Display and briefly introduce several biographies. These books all belong to the same genre, or category, of writing. What is the genre called? *(biographies)* What characteristics make them biographies? *Record students' responses on chart paper. Their responses should include: tells the true story of a real person's life; tells why the person's life is important; can be about someone famous but doesn't have to be; tells about the person's actions, thoughts, feelings, and words; written in the third person; can tell about a person's whole life or part of it.*

To write a biography, writers need to do a lot of research. Writers often spend months collecting information before they ever begin to write. What are some ways a biographer might learn about his or her subject? *List students' answers on chart paper. Their responses should include: interviews with the subject and with people who knew him or her; books; newspapers; letters; speeches or quotes; diaries; and photographs.*

A biographer often expresses opinions or makes judgments about his or her subject based on the facts he or she finds during research. Russell Freedman says that when he writes a biography, "I choose a person I admire. I don't know if I would ever want to write about someone I didn't admire. It means in a sense that I live with that person for a year. I go to bed at night thinking about that person and I wake up in the morning thinking about him or her." (*Author Talk,* Section 4)

Have students brainstorm a list of possible subjects for a biography. Write their ideas on chart paper. Then have students choose a subject and list some possible research sources.

Practicing the Skill

Have students locate some research sources in the school library on the subject of their biography. Then have students write a few paragraphs about what they find interesting about their subject. This can be used as a first step for a longer biographical piece.

You Will Need

- chart paper
- access to the school library or enough biographies for all students to choose one
- several interesting, well-written biographies (see Teacher Tip)

Teacher Tip

Examples of interesting, well-written biographies:

- *Abigail Adams: Witness to a Revolution* by Natalie S. Bober
- *Anthony Burns: The Defeat and Triumph of a Fugitive Slave* by Virginia Hamilton
- *The Double Life of Pocahontas* by Jean Fritz
- *The Life and Death of Crazy Horse* by Russell Freedman

Assessment Connection

First evaluate students' choices for biographical research. Will sources be readily available? Then read students' paragraphs about their subjects. Did they include information that their readers would find interesting? For students having difficulty with biographical research, suggest that they choose a subject they know and interview him or her.

Writing an Essay: Identifying Facts and Opinions

You Will Need

- transparency markers
- overhead projector
- overhead transparencies of BLM 34 and BLM 34A ("The Case for Sneakers" and "America's Favorite Shoe")
- a collection of books that have opinions expressed by several contributors such as ones compiled by Michelle Roehm

Lesson Background

Students are constantly sharing opinions on many subjects. They also express their views in writing. This mini-lesson helps students understand the difference between fact and opinion and the need to support their viewpoints with factual details.

Teaching the Lesson

1. Display "The Case for Sneakers" on the overhead projector and read it with students. Then display and read "America's Favorite Shoe." Ask students to identify similarities and differences between the two pieces.

2. Remind students that a fact is something that can be proven and an opinion expresses the writer's thoughts or beliefs and cannot be proven.

3. Help students determine that the first essay mainly expresses opinion. The second essay expresses an opinion that is supported by facts. Point out that an opinion essay is improved by including facts that support the writer's point of view.

4. Have students note that the writer of "America's Favorite Shoe" began the essay by stating an opinion and then provided facts to support that opinion. Invite student volunteers to identify the opinions in the piece by underlining them in one color. Have them underline the facts used to support the opinions in another color. Mention that writers sometimes provide facts first and then state an opinion based on those facts.

5. Suggest a current classroom, school, or community issue. Ask students to jot down an opinion about the issue. Group students with similar opinions about the issue. Give groups three minutes to brainstorm supporting facts for their opinions. Provide time for sharing.

Assessment Connection

Review students' essays to determine whether students have supported their opinions with appropriate facts. Conduct individual conferences with students who are having difficulty distinguishing facts from opinions. Ask them to bring to the conference a piece of writing that expresses an opinion. Have them identify the opinions and the facts in the same way the class completed the exercise in #4 under Teaching the Lesson.

Practicing the Skill

- Ask each student to use the topic from the group work or select another issue and draft an opinion essay supported with facts.

- Read selected pages from books that have opinions expressed from various contributors. Two very good examples are *Boys Know It All* and *Girls Know Best*, both compiled by Michelle Roehm. Ask students to determine whether the opinions you read are supported by facts.

- Have students examine letters to the editor in a local newspaper. Have them identify the letter writer's opinion statements and supporting details.

Writing Essays: Supporting Opinions with Evidence

Lesson Background

An effective opinion essay stands on a solid foundation of evidence, including both facts and examples. In this mini-lesson, students learn to use facts and examples to support opinion statements.

Teaching the Lesson

1. Tell students that you are going to read them the beginning of an essay that you are writing.

> The best kinds of books are mystery books because they have something to please everyone. Most mystery books make you eager to keep reading. One way mystery authors hook your attention is by ending chapters at suspenseful points. For instance, Chapter One of Who Really Killed Cock Robin? by Jean Craighead George ends with the main character being challenged to solve the mystery of the death of the town's mascot.
>
> Mysteries are also fun because they make you think. As you read along, you try to figure out what is going to happen next as you try to solve the mystery.
>
> I am not the only one who thinks mysteries are entertaining. When I asked other teachers how they felt, seven out of twelve said they love reading mysteries.

2. Make a two-column chart on the board or on chart paper. Write "Show Me the Evidence" at the top of the chart. Use the following headings for the columns: *Facts* and *Examples*. Review the definitions of the terms: Facts are things that are true or can be proven. Examples are words, phrases, and sentences that offer proof—they are the evidence. Then explain to students that you used evidence to back up your opinion that mysteries are fun. Ask them to identify the facts and examples in your essay. Write students' responses in the appropriate columns. Ask, "What other evidence could you use in supporting your opinion about mystery books?"

3. Ask students what kind of reading they most enjoy. Have them plan the facts and examples they will use to support their opinions by making their own "Show Me the Evidence" charts.

Practicing the Skill

Have students write opinion essays based on their "Show Me the Evidence" charts.

You Will Need

- chart paper
- markers
- highlighters

Revising Tip

After students have drafted opinion pieces, ask them to use different-colored highlighters to color-code the kinds of evidence they have included—facts and examples. If they find that they have relied too heavily on one type of evidence, encourage students to provide more balanced evidence in their final copy.

Assessment Connection

Review students' completed "Show Me the Evidence" charts to ensure that they have included both facts and examples. As you read students' essays, check to see that they have incorporated a balance of facts and examples. Meet with students who are having difficulty supporting opinion statements with evidence. Help them complete a "Show Me the Evidence" chart for another piece they have written to reinforce the concept.

Writing an Essay: Using Questionnaires

Lesson Background

Effective writers back up their opinions with evidence. One kind of evidence is statistics. In this mini-lesson, students learn how to formulate survey questions, conduct research, and include the resulting statistics in an opinion essay.

Teaching the Lesson

Statistics are facts in number form. For example, one statistic is that there are _____ girls and _____ boys in our class. *(Give appropriate numbers.)* Sometimes it is hard to find statistics related to an opinion essay you want to write. However, you may be able to take a survey and do your own study. For example, if I wanted to write an essay about my opinion that most students enjoy outdoor recess more than indoor recess, I would survey students in our school. I could ask a few students from each class.

First, I would decide on a question such as, "Do you prefer indoor or outdoor recess?" Then, I would create a form for collecting the answers or data. *Show the Survey Questionnaire Form on chart paper.* After I had all the information from my survey, I would use it as one part of my evidence. For example, I might write: My opinion that students prefer outdoor recess is supported by the fact that 20 of 35 children surveyed said they liked outdoor recess better.

SURVEY QUESTIONNAIRE FORM

Survey Question: Do you prefer indoor or outdoor recess?

Grade	Indoor	Outdoor
3	ЦЖ I	ЦЖ II
4	ЦЖ I	ЦЖ I
5	III	ЦЖ II

Now you will have a turn to create your own questionnaire. Think of an opinion that could be supported by surveying people you know. Use a form like the one I showed, or make up your own.

Practicing the Skill

Have students do additional research to find facts to support their opinions. Then have them write an opinion essay. Tell students to incorporate statistics from their survey along with the other evidence they have collected.

Teacher Tip

Point out that in some cases, survey results may fail to support students' opinions. This situation provides students an opportunity to do further research and to possibly rethink their opinions.

Assessment Connection

Check that students have created clear survey questions that directly relate to their opinion statements. Note whether students' completed essays incorporate the statistics they gathered. For students who are having difficulty gathering statistics, review the Survey Questionnaire Form you showed them earlier and ask: "How can you use this form to record the answers to your survey question? Will changing your question in some way help you get the information you want?"

Writing Informative Texts: Writing Nonfiction Reports and Books

Lesson Background

"We do not write what we know; we write what we want to find out," nonfiction author Wallace Stegner notes. Writers research topics that interest them and then communicate what they learn through their writing. Students have written informative reports in previous grades. This mini-lesson builds on that background as they write longer reports in book form.

Teaching the Lesson

1. Tell students that you want to write a book about kites. Draw a Web on chart paper. On each of three branches, write a subtopic to investigate: *History of kites; Uses of kites;* and *New techniques in kite making.*

2. Make a KWL chart for the first of your three subtopics. Brainstorm with students to record their prior knowledge in the *Know* column and their questions in the *Want to Know* column. Explain that you will do research to answer your questions, and that you will record the answers in the *Learn* column. Make similar KWL charts for your other two subtopics.

3. Tell students that you will use what you learned to write a nonfiction book about kites, and explain that the information on each KWL chart will be the basis of a chapter.

   Review the use of paragraphs to organize nonfiction writing. (See Mini-lesson 27.) Tell students that each chapter will include an introductory paragraph, at least one body paragraph, and a concluding paragraph. Explain that you will also create introductory and concluding chapters.

4. Ask students to choose a subject to research. Have them create webs to show the three subtopics they want to investigate.

Practicing the Skill

Have students create KWL charts for each of their web subtopics. Guide them in locating resources to answer their questions. Have students take notes on their charts and use this information to create chapters of three to five paragraphs each. Then help students bind their writing into books.

You Will Need

- Web (*Rigby Literacy Graphic Organizer Book,* p. 29)
- KWL Chart (*Rigby Literacy Graphic Organizer Book,* p. 49)
- chart paper
- marker
- art materials for binding books

Assessment Connection

Create an assessment checklist for this project.
- **Introductory chapter presents the topic and subtopics in an interesting way.**
- **Body chapters each include introductory paragraph, one to three body paragraphs, and concluding paragraph. Each paragraph has a main idea supported by details.**
- **Concluding chapter summarizes the information and leaves the reader with an interesting thought or question.**

For students who might have trouble writing longer pieces, you might want to create a small group and have each student contribute one chapter.

Writing Informative Text: Creating an Itinerary

You Will Need

- chart paper
- a marker
- a collection of guidebooks and brochures for local sites

Teacher Tip

Show students how to use an Internet site such as www.mapquest.com to plan the route for their trip.

Assessment Connection

Have each group present and explain their itinerary charts to the class. Note whether the elements of the plans are practical. Is there enough time for each destination? Are all blocks of time accounted for? Is anything confusing about the schedule? For those students who need additional help in creating schedules, have them write an itinerary of a typical school day.

Lesson Background

Learning to use their time wisely is an important skill for fifth graders to develop. At this age, many students have difficulty budgeting time appropriately and effectively. In this mini-lesson, students create an itinerary for a class trip, which helps them use writing to practice time management.

Teaching the Lesson

Let's plan a class trip. *(This can be a real or an imagined trip. Ideally, the trip should relate to a content area unit.)* To get the most out of our trip, we will research places to go and plan how to use our time. The tool we will use to plan is an "itinerary," a special schedule used for trips.

Where can we find information about places to go? *Record responses on chart paper. Students may suggest guidebooks, Web sites, brochures, the telephone, and e-mail conversations.*

Imagine that we decided to go to the Colonial History Museum. We would look through materials to find out about the museum displays. Once we have ideas about what to see, we can write our itinerary. *Make a three-column chart on chart paper. Write the heading "Colonial History Museum" with the column headings* Time, Exhibit/Area, What to See and Learn.

Let's plan to arrive at 9:30. *Write 9:30 in the first column.* Imagine that we want to see the old schoolhouse exhibit first. *Write* Old Schoolhouse Exhibit *in the middle column.* What might we want to learn at that exhibit? *Elicit students' responses, and write them in the third column on the chart.* We should plan to spend 20 minutes there. Then we would write *9:50* on the next line of our chart and decide what to do next.

Present a collection of guidebooks and brochures. You will work in groups to plan your own trip. Each group will select a place to visit, create an itinerary chart, and list sources of information about the place.

Practicing the Skill

- Have students use their itinerary charts to plan class trips. Ask groups to present their ideas to the class. If possible, choose one of the destinations for an actual class trip.

- Point out that an itinerary is a type of schedule. Suggest that schedules can be helpful in keeping track of other activities, including major school assignments and after-school activities.

Business Letters: Writing Clear Explanations

Lesson Background

Students at this level often have difficulty writing with purpose, focus, and clarity. In this mini-lesson, students practice these skills by writing business letters that contain clear explanations.

Teaching the Lesson

1. Write the following on chart paper:

   Terry Evans, President
   Wonder Toy Company
   1 Ross Road
   New York, NY 10000

   Dear Mr. Evans:
       I am returning the Science Wonder Puzzle I bought from you. Please take care of this matter for me.

                   Sincerely,
                   Pat Warner

2. Tell students to read the letter. Ask, "What is missing from this business letter?" (an explanation) Have students list the questions they would have if they were Mr. Evans.

3. Display the transparency. Ask students to note the explanation provided in the letter. Point out that whether a writer of a business letter wants to order a product, get money back, receive information, or have a suggestion considered, a clear explanation is essential.

4. Brainstorm a list of businesses students have contact with, such as local retail stores, restaurants, movie theaters, and so on. Then ask students to think of a purpose for writing to one of these businesses, such as an inquiry about when a popular movie will come to the theater, or a menu suggestion for a restaurant. Have students write drafts of business letters that clearly explain *why* they are writing and *what* they would like to have happen as a result of their letter.

Practicing the Skill

Tell students that another type of business letter is a complimentary letter. Ask each student to think of a product or a service that he or she would like to say good things about. Ask them to write business letters that clearly tell *what* their compliment is and *why* they are offering it. Also, help students determine whom the recipient of their letter should be.

You Will Need

- overhead projector
- overhead transparency of BLM 39 (Business Letter)
- chart paper
- marker

Teacher Tip

Have students use *Putting It in Writing* by Steve Otfinoski as a reference for form and style when they are writing business letters.

Assessment Connection

Check students' business letters to be sure they include clear explanations, including *what* and *why* details. If they do not, ask students questions in individual conferences to elicit the missing information.

Writing Business Letters: Memos and Notices

Lesson Background

Memos are a form of written communication that can be useful to students as they participate in school and community activities. In this mini-lesson, students learn to write effective memos.

Teaching the Lesson

1. Display the transparency. Read the memo aloud. Have students note and discuss the purpose of each part of the memo. Ask students to compare the format of a memo to that of a standard business letter.

2. List the following purposes for memos on chart paper: *explanation, notice, request, suggestion, complaint,* and *opinion.* Have students identify the purpose of the memo you read. (notice)

3. Read aloud a few memos you have received in school or at home. Ask students to identify the purposes of the memos. Have them identify characteristics that the memos have in common, such as shortness in length; identification of the date, audience, writer, and subject; a businesslike tone; a clear outline of the topic; suggestions for how to get more information; and so on. Record their responses on chart paper with the heading "Effective Memos." Display the list in the classroom as a resource for students.

4. Have each student write a memo about an event or activity that will take place in your classroom. The memo may be written to the principal, parents, or another class. Help students distribute the completed memos.

Practicing the Skill

- Have students write memos that compliment, express a concern, or make a suggestion to the publisher of one of their textbooks.

- Collect memos on appropriate topics and ask groups to evaluate them based on the "Effective Memos" chart the class created.

You Will Need

- overhead projector
- overhead transparency of BLM 40 (Memo)
- collection of memos
- chart paper
- marker

Teacher Tip

Remind students that memos, while briefer and less formal than business letters, must still follow the rules of good writing.

Revising Tip

At the peer review stage, have students focus on clarity in their writing. Have partners jot down any questions they have about the content of the memo while writers read their memos aloud.

Assessment Connection

Evaluate students' completed memos based on their purpose, content, clarity, language, and grammar. For students who need additional help writing memos, provide models of effective memos as references.

Writing Nonfiction: Investigating and Using Graphic Features

Lesson Background

By fifth grade, students are ready to add new elements to nonfiction writing. This mini-lesson encourages students to include graphic features in their writing as a way to communicate information to their readers.

Teaching the Lesson

1. Explain that nonfiction authors often present information in many ways. One method is informational text. But authors also use graphic features in their books—things like maps, charts, tables, and diagrams. Arrange students in small groups and offer each group a nonfiction book. Have them survey the books to locate and identify graphic features. Ask a representative of each group to share two or three examples from the group's book.

2. Display the graphic feature transparency on an overhead projector. Identify the source of the graphic and the topic of the text in which it appears. Guide students to analyze the graphic in terms of content, how information is communicated, and text such as captions, headings, labels, and so on. Then ask students to discuss why they think the graphic is or is not an effective way to present that information.

3. Brainstorm reasons why a nonfiction writer might choose to use a graphic feature rather than paragraphs. For example, it is much more understandable to show readers where Mt. Everest is on a map than to try to explain its location in words. And a labeled diagram of mountain-climbing gear presents that information more efficiently than text would.

4. Ask students to look through their portfolios to select nonfiction writing they have been working on. Have them reread their work and identify information that could be presented as a graphic feature rather than text, or information that could be enhanced by including a graphic. Have them make notes about the type of feature they would use and the information it would communicate.

Practicing the Skill

Ask students to use their notes to create graphic features to include in revisions of their nonfiction writing. Remind them that their graphic features should contain text in the form of captions, labels, headings, and so on.

You Will Need

- informational books that include graphic features such as charts, tables, maps, photographs, illustrations, and diagrams
- transparency of a graphic feature from one book

Assessment Connection

Work with individual students to look at both versions of their nonfiction writing—before and after adding graphic features. Ask students to explain what information they wanted to express graphically and why they chose a particular graphic feature to communicate that information. If a student's graphic feature does not adequately convey the information it was intended to, ask questions to help with revisions; for example, "How can you show the reader what this information on your chart means?"

Writing Nonfiction: Summarizing Research Results

You Will Need

- an overhead transparency of a passage from a nonfiction book
- overhead projector
- transparency marker
- chart paper
- marker

Suggested trade titles:
- *Lincoln: A Photobiography* by Russell Freedman
- *Eating the Plates: A Pilgrim Book of Food and Manners* by Lucille Recht Penner

Assessment Connection

Suggest that students self-assess their summaries by using a checklist with questions like these:
- Did I include all the important ideas?
- Did I write in complete sentences?
- Is the order of my summary logical?
- Did I use my own words?

Lesson Background

When writing informational reports, students are faced with organizing and making sense of great amounts of reading material. This mini-lesson teaches a strategy for organizing the most important information in what students read.

Teaching the Lesson

1. Tell students that when you research a topic, you must do a lot of reading in many different sources. However, sometimes you read so much that it can be hard to remember what you have learned. Explain that one way you can organize your information is by writing a summary of what you learn from a reference.

2. Choose a passage from a nonfiction book that contains a lot of information. Display the passage on an overhead transparency and have students follow along as you read it aloud.

3. Explain to students that before you can write a summary, you must think about what you have read. You need to skim the text again and pick out the most important ideas. Direct volunteers to underline the main points in the passage.

4. Point out to students that when you summarize the passage, you want to include all the underlined ideas. Emphasize that you won't copy the information exactly but will write it in your own words in an order that makes sense to you.

5. Together with students, write a one-paragraph summary of the passage on chart paper.

6. Think about a topic you would like to research. Read a passage that tells about that topic. Then write a one-paragraph summary of the passage. Remember to include only the most important information.

Practicing the Skill

Ask students to each write a summary of material they have recently read in a content-area text. Have them share their summaries with partners to compare the most important points they identified from the text.

Writing a Newspaper Article: Choosing an Audience

Lesson Background

By fifth grade, writers should be able to identify their audience. This mini-lesson helps students consider the backgrounds and interests of their readers so they can tailor newspaper articles to appeal to various audiences.

Teaching the Lesson

1. Tell students they will read two newspaper articles about the same event. Cover the source of each article before presenting it. Display BLM 43 and then BLM 43A, having students read both articles.

2. Ask students to name the audience for whom they think each article was written. Ask them to explain why they think that. Uncover the source of each article. Guide students to the conclusion that both articles convey essentially the same information, but that the first article is written for parents while the second is written for students.

3. Point out that writers must consider the specific audience for which they are writing. They must think about what the reader already knows about the topic as well as what words and ideas will have to be explained. They must also consider what information will interest their readers.

4. Divide the class into groups of five. Assign each group an event or issue related to the community. Allow some time for group discussion of the assigned topic. Have each group member draw a card with one of the following audiences written on it: *parents, teachers, first graders, middle school students,* and *grandparents.* Instruct each student to jot down what a person in his or her assigned audience would know and need to know about the topic. Have students use a "Know/Need to Know" chart for their notes.

5. Have students draft a newspaper article about their group's event or issue for the audience whose card they drew. Remind them to use their charts when drafting their articles.

Practicing the Skill

Give students opportunities to write for specific audiences in other formats. Have students choose a content area topic such as pioneers or explorers. Brainstorm different writing formats—reports, stories, poems, and more. Then choose several audiences—first graders, another fifth-grade class, and parents, for example. Have each student choose a format and audience to write for. Let them share their finished work with the intended audiences.

You Will Need

- overhead projector
- overhead transparencies of BLM 43 and BLM 43A (News Articles)
- cards with role assignments

Teacher Tip

Tell students that writer John Steinbeck suggested, "I have found that sometimes it helps to pick out one person—a real person you know, or an imagined person, and to write to that one." Encourage students to try this technique in their writing and to discuss their feelings about how effective it is.

Assessment Connection

Check for students' attempts to appeal to a particular audience. Did they provide appropriate background information where necessary? Did they make any incorrect or unintentional assumptions in their writing? Have students who need extra support write an article for a specific classmate about something they know well. Before beginning to write, have students interview their readers to find out what they know and don't know about the topic. Then help them write their articles with the specific needs of their readers in mind.

Writing Newspaper Articles: Using Concise Sentences

You Will Need

- chart paper
- marker
- newspaper article

Revising Tip

Tell students that newspaper and magazine editors often ask writers to revise their writing to make it fit a certain space. Have students revisit a nonfiction piece they have written. Challenge them to shorten the piece while retaining its meaning.

Publishing Power

Have students use their brainstormed lists to draft an article for a classroom newsletter.

Assessment Connection

As students draft their newspaper articles, note whether they are using clear, direct language. You may want to impose word count limits on students who tend toward wordiness in their writing.

Lesson Background

Writer William Strunk, Jr. once wrote, "A sentence should contain no unnecessary words for the same reason that a machine should have no unnecessary parts." Young writers often need to be reminded that long, complex sentences and overuse of modifiers can complicate simple ideas. This mini-lesson helps students learn to write clear, concise sentences.

Teaching the Lesson

1. Write the sentence below on chart paper and have students read it aloud.

   Today the students of the fifth-grade class and I will labor toward the goal of making our written communication a model of clarity and conciseness.

2. Ask students to comment on the sentence and to suggest ways in which it might be revised to make it clearer and shorter.

   Then ask, "What do you notice when you compare the two sentences? Why did we make the changes we did? What did we eliminate?" Help students recognize that the structure of the first sentence was too complicated and that long phrases and complicated words were used in places where simpler, more concise words and phrases would make the message clearer.

3. Tell students that newspaper writers must write concisely so that their readers get clear information quickly and easily. Also, explain that newspaper writers usually have only a limited amount of space for their articles.

4. Read aloud a short newspaper article that is written clearly and concisely. Ask students, "How did the writer make the article clear and brief? What details were included? What kind of information was left out and why?"

5. In small groups, ask students to choose an interesting event that has happened to the class. Provide several minutes for them to brainstorm all the information they can concerning the event and to record that information. Then have students identify the most important information to include in a brief article.

Practicing the Skill

Distribute copies of a letter to the editor. Have students work in pairs to revise the letter to make it more concise.

Writing to Test Prompts

Lesson Background

In a classroom, students are often allowed to self-select their topic, audience, or writing form. In a testing environment, however, students are usually required to write to specific prompts in which these elements are assigned. This mini-lesson teaches techniques for successfully responding to writing prompts.

Teaching the Lesson

1. Display the chart paper with the first writing prompt. Tell students that this prompt is similar to ones they see on writing tests. Explain that one way to organize their thoughts when responding to a writing prompt is the TAP-F technique. Write the following TAP-F headings below the writing prompt, leaving space for writing after each heading.

   Topic _____

   Audience _____

   Purpose _____

   Form _____

2. Have students read the prompt carefully. Work together to fill in the TAP-F chart. Explain that filling in a TAP-F chart for a test writing prompt makes it easier to write exactly as required.

3. Explain that the QAD technique is another way to plan a response to a writing prompt. Write the following on chart paper:

Question	Answer	Details

   Help students identify questions related to the first writing prompt. (What would you do? Why would it be helpful? When would you do it?) Record them on the chart. Have students propose answers and supporting details for each question and record their ideas. Explain that each answer from the chart can be developed into a paragraph in the body of the writing. Then ask students to suggest an introduction and a conclusion for the letter.

Practicing the Skill

Have students use one of the techniques to respond to the second writing prompt. Remind students that they should always reread their writing carefully and make any necessary revisions.

You Will Need

- chart paper
- marker
- the following writing prompts written on chart paper:

Writing Prompt #1
Think of a way that your class could help a first grade class. Think about what you would do, why it would be helpful, and when the project could be done. Now write a letter to explain your ideas to the principal.

Writing Prompt #2
Think of a time when someone you know showed courage. Think about what happened, what the person did, and how people reacted. Now write an essay about the event for your class.

Assessment Connection

Create a scoring rubric to evaluate student responses to writing prompts. Possible questions for the rubric might include: Did the writer direct the piece to the intended audience? Did the writing have a clear topic with supporting details? Did the writer use the writing form specified? Share the rubric with students before they write so that they have a clear understanding of expectations.

Writing Rhythmic Poetry

You Will Need

For Laughing Out Loud: Poems to Tickle Your Funny Bone selected by Jack Prelutsky, or another book of poetry

Teacher Tip

Remind students to focus on meaning and emotion as well as language patterns. Share Robert Frost's words: "There are three things, after all, that a poem must reach: the eye, the ear, and what we may call the heart, or the mind. It is most important of all to reach the heart of the reader." Encourage students to focus on language that will touch the hearts and minds of their readers when writing their poems.

Assessment Connection

Note whether students have used a pattern of rhyme and rhythm while conveying meaning in their poetry. For students who have trouble incorporating rhythm and rhyme into their poetry, have them choose a favorite published poem and model their own after that one.

Lesson Background

"A poet is, before anything else, a person who is passionately in love with language," according to poet W. H. Auden. This mini-lesson teaches students how to work with language patterns to create rhythmic poetry.

Teaching the Lesson

1. Read students a short, rhyming poem with a regular rhythm such as "My Dog" by Mac Fatchen in Jack Prelutsky's collection *For Laughing Out Loud: Poems to Tickle Your Funny Bone.* Ask students what, in addition to humor, makes the poem fun to read and listen to. Help students identify the rhyming pattern.

2. Read the poem again and ask students to focus on its rhythm. Tell students that one way to give poetry a rhythm, or beat, is to use a regular pattern of syllables. Have students count the syllables in each line of Fatchen's poem to discover the pattern he used. (8, 6, 8, 6)

3. Present other poems with regular syllable patterns. Some examples from the same collection are "Bursting" by Dorothy Aldis (8, 8, 8, 8) and "The Ombley-Gombley" by Peter Wesley-Smith (6, 6, 3, 3, 6).

4. Ask students to work in pairs to draft their own rhyming poems with a rhythmic pattern of syllables.

Practicing the Skill

- Have students read a wide variety of poems to observe their rhyme and rhythmic patterns. Two excellent collections are *Tomie dePaola's Book of Poems* and *Sky Scrape/City Scape: Poems of City Life* by Jane Yolen (editor).

- Collect a variety of greeting cards written in verse. Encourage students to examine the rhyme and rhythmic patterns of each one. Then have them make their own poetic cards with art materials or a computer program.

- Create a Poetry Center. Place a tape recorder and cassettes in the station, along with several books of poetry. Ask students to visit the station to record their own poetry and others' poems. Allow students opportunities for listening to the recordings.

Using Reference Tools: The Internet

Lesson Background

Traditionally, students have used reference sources such as encyclopedias, almanacs, and magazines to do much of their research. But today's young writers should also be able to effectively utilize Internet research resources. These tools can be especially useful for checking information or for finding interesting details to add to drafts. This mini-lesson focuses on teaching students how to wisely and efficiently use the resources of the Internet.

Teaching the Lesson

I have drafted an article about Mary McLeod Bethune for our classroom library. In a book, I read that Ms. Bethune started a school in the early 1900s. I want to check an online encyclopedia to see if I can find the exact year. *Demonstrate the use of www.britannica.com to look up* "Mary McLeod Bethune." This encyclopedia states that Ms. Bethune started her school in 1904.

I'd also like to find a Web site that includes information about her school. A search engine is the best way to find information quickly. There are special search engines that are designed just for students. *Demonstrate using www.yahooligans.com to look up* "Mary McLeod Bethune." This says Ms. Bethune started her school with just $1.50. That is an interesting fact I might want to add to my nonfiction writing.

The Internet can also be useful in researching information for fiction writing. For example, if you are writing a story, you may be able to gather details that will help you describe a particular setting.

Review a piece of writing you are working on now, and list ways you might use the Internet to check facts or find information to add to your writing.

Practicing the Skill

- Have pairs of students work together to use the Internet to locate information for their writing. Suggest National Geographic at www.nationalgeographic.com and the Smithsonian Institution at www.si.edu, both good informational sites.

- Have students add useful Internet addresses they find to a "Super Sites" notebook. Use dividers to sort the sites by subject.

You Will Need

computers with Internet access

Teacher Tip

- Talk with students about Internet safety. Impress upon them the importance of not providing any personal information as they visit sites.
- Remind students they must give credit when they use information from the Internet just as they cite the authors of books and magazines they use as resources. Show students the bibliographic format you want them to use.

Assessment Connection

To assess students' Internet search techniques, ask pairs of students to go online. Have one student identify information to locate. Have the other student write down the steps and key words his or her partner uses to locate information. Then have students switch roles. Review students' notes to determine the need for additional instruction.

Rereading Your Work

You Will Need

- overhead projector
- overhead transparency of description of Ashley Bryan (see Teaching the Lesson)
- overhead marking pen
- tape recorder
- blank tapes

Teacher Tip

On a "Helpful Experts" chart, invite students to sign their names and indicate what type of help they may be able to provide for fellow writers.

Assessment Connection

During writing conferences, note improvements students have made as a result of rereading their work. Observe whether students in peer conferences ask specific questions of classmates.

Lesson Background

Effective writers know how to reread their own work and how to get help from others. This mini-lesson helps students reread and revise.

Teaching the Lesson

1. First explain to students that writers reread their work. Tell students that rereading can help a writer find places to make improvements to his or her writing. Ideas may be added, cut, or switched around. Sentences may be cut or rewritten. Interesting language and vivid descriptions can be added. Then model rereading for students. Display the transparency and read the text as if you had no audience.

2. Tell the students that you will now reread your work, bit by bit.

   Author Ashley Bryan's parents were from the West Indies. Ashley and his brothers and sisters grew up in New York, though.

   "The beginning is dull. I'll ask (student from your class) for help. She/He has creative ideas." Write, "Ask _____." by the first sentence.

   The family loved reading but did not have money for books. The children checked out books from the library. They put them on shelves made of boxes and pretended they had their own library.

   "'They put them' is confusing. I will change it to 'They put the books.'"

   Ashley still thinks it is important to be surrounded by books. When he visits classrooms, he tells children to save extra coins in jars to buy books.

   "I want to mention some of Mr. Bryan's books. I will ask our librarian because he/she may know this author's works."

3. Then, ask students to reread one of their first drafts. Have them write three questions about their work and write the name of a classmate or resource person they might ask about their writing.

Practicing the Skill

At an audiotaping center, record each student rereading part of a first draft and thinking aloud about changes to be made. Make the tapes available for the class to listen to. A week after this lesson, ask students to share revisions they have made after rereading.

Conferencing with Teachers and Peers

Lesson Background

As students mature as writers, they are able to make increasingly good use of peer and teacher review. They are also better able to decide which suggestions to follow and which to disregard. In this mini-lesson, students learn how to take part in writing discussions similar to those that professional writers participate in with editors and other writers.

Teaching the Lesson

1. Have students recall and share previous experiences with peer conferencing. Mention that some professional writers meet in homes, libraries, or restaurants to share encouragement and feedback. Explain that these meetings are similar to peer conferences.

2. Explain that writers often depend on two groups of people to help them with their writing—other writers and editors. Ask students to share any prior knowledge about the role of magazine and book editors. Tell students that editors help writers make their writing the best it can be. Point out that teacher conferences are similar to writer-editor conferences. These meetings help writers clarify guidelines and get new ideas about their approach to writing.

3. Share the following quote by Stephen Manes: "Editors may make suggestions, but ultimately the book is your handiwork, your creation." Point out that writers may disregard suggestions from others if they have clear, logical reasons for doing so.

4. Introduce the following chart to show students how, why, and where to get input about their writing.

Problem	Editor or Writing Group?	Responses	Change or Not?

Have students create their own charts. Then ask them to choose a current piece of writing and identify some problems they are having with it. Ask them to think about how they can use the chart to get input about how to solve those problems.

Practicing the Skill

After students have created their charts and listed some problems they are having with a piece of writing, help them schedule editorial conferences with you or writing group conferences with peers.

You Will Need

- chart paper
- marker

Teacher Tip

Consider supervising an optional writing group during lunch or providing snacks for students who wish to participate in an after-school group.

Assessment Connection

Review student's charts to determine if they are able to identify problems in their writing and then make changes suggested by peers or you. When students indicate on their charts that they will *not* make particular changes that were suggested, ask them to jot down their reasons. Suggest that if they are unable to explain a reason, they should consider making the change to see how it affects their writing.

Making Decisions About Word Choices

Lesson Background

"All the fun's in how you say a thing," believed Robert Frost. Rather than see revision as a chore, students can view it as a welcome opportunity to experiment with language and to play with words. In this mini-lesson, students learn how word choice can affect the message and mood of their writing.

Teaching the Lesson

1. Tell students that writers often struggle with finding words that accurately describe what they are trying to say.

2. Display the sentences you prepared, but mask the second sentence. Ask students to read the first sentence. Have a volunteer describe the image the sentence brings to mind. Then display the second sentence and have students identify the differences between the two versions (specific noun, vivid verb, sensory adjective). Have them tell how these differences affect their mental images. Guide students to realize that the word choices in the second version make the sentence show rather than tell what is happening.

3. Help students understand that each word they use in their writing conveys a specific meaning, and that they should always choose their words carefully. Point out that a dictionary and a thesaurus are building blocks for writers. Help students understand that they can use these resources to choose words that will convey their meaning clearly.

4. Ask students to select pieces of writing from their portfolios. Have pairs meet to brainstorm word changes that would make their writing more interesting and precise. Make sure each student has a dictionary and a thesaurus for this activity.

Practicing the Skill

- Have students underline descriptive adjectives and adverbs in a piece of writing they are revising. Ask them to consider how to replace some of these words with more precise nouns and vivid verbs that communicate the same meaning.

- Have students use their writer's notebooks to keep a word bank of precise nouns and vivid verbs from other writers' works. Suggest that they review these lists periodically to help them make their own writing more interesting.

Editing: Adding Details or Other Information

Lesson Background

You have probably experienced the frustration of a poor connection during a phone conversation—with words or sentences garbled or missing. The same frustration results when reading something in which key information has been left out. This mini-lesson helps students discover and address information gaps in their writing.

Teaching the Lesson

When you are writing a story or nonfiction piece, you need to make sure that all the information the reader needs is included. What types of information or details should a writer include in a piece of writing? *Elicit responses such as sensory details to help the reader picture a scene, details that support the main idea, clear explanations and descriptions, and so on.*

I am going to read the beginning of an article I am writing about reindeer. As you listen, think about information I may have left out. Jot down any questions that you have. *Read the following passage aloud.*

> You may have heard of magical reindeer, but how much do you know about real reindeer? These animals are similar to deer, but their antlers make them different. They are also unique because of the special food they eat. It helps them survive the harsh Arctic winters.

Display the chart you prepared. What questions do you have about this passage? *Record students' responses in the left-hand column of the chart. Questions may include the following: What makes their antlers different? What do they eat? How does it help them survive?*

Answering these questions will make my writing clearer and more interesting. When I revise my writing, I can include information like this. *Record ideas such as the following in the right-hand column: Both males and females have antlers. They eat moss. The moss works like antifreeze to keep their insides from freezing.*

Now choose a piece of writing you are working on, and exchange it with a partner. Read each other's work and list questions that you would like answered in the piece or suggestions for information that could be added during revisions.

Practicing the Skill

Have students return the drafts and lists of questions and suggestions to their partners. Ask them to use this information to revise their drafts by adding details that fill in the gaps.

You Will Need

- markers
- the following chart written on chart paper:

Question	What I Need to Add

Revising Tip

Suggest that students reread their writing aloud after adding the details suggested by their partners. Ask them to be sure that the added information flows smoothly into the piece without sounding "tacked on."

Assessment Connection

As you read students' writing, record on sticky notes the questions that you think the piece needs to answer. Place these notes in the margins near where information or details need to be added. Follow up with students to see that they have added the appropriate material in their revisions.

Editing: Trying New Techniques and Approaches

Lesson Background

Early writing experiences focus on the basics of selecting topics, organizing ideas, and learning how to elaborate. As students mature, they begin to explore more creative ways of expressing themselves. This mini-lesson uses writing samples to encourage young authors to experiment with new techniques and approaches in their own writing.

Teaching the Lesson

1. Point out that one way writers get inspiration is by looking at how other writers approach their topics in new and unusual ways. Explain that the goal is not to copy the writer's work, but to think about different ways to express their own ideas.

2. Present a variety of writing techniques such as those that are used in the examples listed below. Have students discuss the technique or approach used by each author and how effective or appealing it is to them as readers.

   - *Henry Reed, Inc.* by Keith Robertson (journal)
   - *Paul Revere's Ride* by Henry Wadsworth Longfellow (narrative poem)
   - *Cuadros de familia/Family Pictures* by Carmen Lomas Garza (bilingual picture book)
   - *Sugaring Time* by Kathryn Lasky (photo-essay)
   - *Shh! We're Writing the Constitution* by Jean Fritz (narrative history)
   - *Eyewitness: Civil War* by John Stanchak (illustrations with captions and short text passages)

3. Arrange students in small groups. Have them take turns sharing current drafts that they would like to revise. Ask group members to brainstorm new approaches each writer could try as a fresh approach to writing.

Practicing the Skill

- Have students revise their drafts using one of the new techniques or approaches suggested in their groups.

- Ask students to look for unusual approaches to fiction and nonfiction in their own reading. Provide time each week for students to share and discuss these approaches and how they can incorporate them into their own writing.

Editing: Deleting Details or Other Unnecessary Information

Lesson Background

Kurt Vonnegut, Jr. advises, "Don't put anything in a story that does not reveal character or advance the action." Student writers often ignore this advice and include unnecessary information in their writing. This mini-lesson helps students consider what details and information should be deleted during revision.

Teaching the Lesson

Mark Twain once said, "A successful book is not made of what is in it, but what is left out of it." When you write, you often include unnecessary information or details that detract from the purpose of your piece. Let's think about the kind of information you don't need in your writing.

Close your eyes. Imagine a garden along the front of a house. See bushes with shiny green leaves brushing against the house. In front of the bushes are beautiful flowers in brilliant reds and yellows. Clumps of tall grass grow among the flowers, hiding some blooms. Dandelions are sprinkled throughout the garden, and poison ivy vines wrap around the bushes. Saplings have sprouted from acorns buried by squirrels.

What does this garden need? *(weeding)* What harm are the weeds causing? *(overshadowing flowers, choking bushes, ruining the design)* How does this garden image relate to writing? *(Things that don't belong spoil the writing.)*

Display the transparency and have students read the passage. What can be "weeded out" of this piece? *Accept students' ideas about information to delete and cross out the unnecessary details. Then reread the passage out loud.*

In small groups, make lists of the kind of information that you should weed out of your writing. For example, you might take out information that does not help establish character or setting, or details that are irrelevant to the plot or topic.

Practicing the Skill

Have students use the lists they created in their groups to "weed out" unnecessary details or information in a piece of writing they are currently revising.

You Will Need

- transparency marker
- overhead projector
- transparency of BLM 53 (Deleting Unnecessary Information)

Assessment Connection

After reading a student's fiction piece, place question marks next to dialogue and descriptions that may not be necessary. After reading a nonfiction piece, put a check by each detail that supports the main idea. Put a question mark by details that do not support the main idea. Review your marks with students in individual conferences and discuss how deleting those details might affect the work.

Editing: Moving Text

You Will Need

- marker
- the following text written on chart paper:

Ida Lewis took over her father's job as lighthouse keeper in 1857. At the time, it was a very unusual job for a woman. In 1869 she rowed out to save two soldiers whose boat had overturned in a storm. In the late 1850s, she rescued four men from the sea. Ida was only fifteen years old when she became a lighthouse keeper. It took twenty-two years for the government to give her that title officially.

Assessment Connection

When reviewing student drafts and revisions, look for evidence that moving text was considered—and occasionally used—during revisions. If some students forget to use the technique, work with them individually to determine how moving text might improve their writing. As changes are suggested, help students mark their writing to reflect the changes they want to make.

Lesson Background

In *Shoptalk: Learning to Write with Writers,* Donald Murray says that writers look at revision and editing as the opportunity "to go to work to make it work." This mini-lesson gives students the opportunity to practice a useful tool for making their own writing work—moving text around so that the final piece is stronger and clearer.

Teaching the Lesson

1. Point out that students aren't the only writers who spend time revising and editing their work. Even professional writers reread, revise, and rewrite repeatedly. Explain that they use many techniques in the revision process—adding details, changing words, trying new approaches, and so on. Tell students that another method used by writers is moving text around.

2. Display the paragraph on chart paper, and have students read it. Explain that you are thinking about moving some of the text to make the writing clearer and more powerful. Ask for their suggestions on how to do so. Help students recognize that the writing will be clearer if the two rescues are mentioned in chronological order; and that it might be more powerful to lead with the most interesting facts—that Ida became a lighthouse keeper at fifteen and that the government didn't recognize her as such for twenty-two years.

3. Demonstrate for students how to mark the text to show how you want to move things around. Show students how to use circles and arrows and the transpose proofreading symbol.

4. Have students look at a draft of their own writing that is ready for revision. Ask them to consider how moving text might improve their work. Have them use circles, arrows, and proofreading symbols to indicate which text they want to move and where they want to move it.

Practicing the Skill

- Ask students to rewrite their drafts with the text in the revised positions. Then have them compare the draft and the revision to see if moving the text helped to improve the piece.

- Explain that some writers physically move text. They cut a draft apart and move things around until the order seems right; then they tape or paste the moved text in its new position. Have students try this with another piece of their writing. Afterward, ask volunteers to explain which method works best for them and why.

Tools for Revision: Proofreading Symbols

Lesson Background

Author Robert Cormier says, "The beautiful part of writing is that you don't have to get it right the first time, unlike say, a brain surgeon." However, when writers reach the proofreading stage, it is time to focus on correcting errors. This mini-lesson reviews proofreading symbols and helps students understand that proofreading and revision are important steps in helping writers "get it right."

Teaching the Lesson

1. Write the proofreading symbols found on page 48 of the *Writer's Handbook* on chart paper. Ask, "What do these marks mean?" After students have identified the symbols, ask, "How do writers use these symbols?" Help students understand that proofreading symbols are a tool writers use to review their work to be sure it is error-free.

2. Display the following text passage on an overhead transparency. Ask volunteers to use proofreading symbols to indicate changes that should be made to the text.

   A still night. Rita looked out her bedroom window. "I don't never remember it snowing in Oct.," she thought. The first snowfall always filled her with a lonely feeling she went back to her desk to do her homework.

3. Ask each student to proofread a piece of his or her own writing, using the symbols to mark the changes that are needed.

Practicing the Skill

- Ask students to use the proofreading symbols to indicate changes they want to make at every stage of rereading and revising their work.

- Point out that in addition to proofreading their own work, many writers depend on professional proofreaders to take a fresh look at their writing. Encourage students to work with partners to exchange writing they have proofread and act as proofreaders for one another by checking for things the writer may have missed.

You Will Need

- *Writer's Handbook*
- chart paper
- markers
- overhead projector
- transparency marker
- transparency with text passage (see Teaching the Lesson)

Teacher Tip

Invite a copyeditor from a local newspaper, magazine, or publishing house to visit the class. Have him or her show examples of marked-up drafts and talk with students about the importance of proofreading.

Assessment Connection

Collect students' marked drafts and subsequent revisions to check whether they are using proofreading symbols effectively. Identify symbols that are used incorrectly or rarely and provide reteaching as needed.

Checking Grammar and Usage

You Will Need

- chart paper
- markers
- overhead projector
- transparency marker
- overhead transparency with the following text:

Luis and Ben walked up to the old house slowly. The garden was tangled with thorny vines. The bricks of the walk was broken. The boys get to the door. Luis looks at Ben as if to say, "You go first." The boys gasped when they herd a loud shriek from inside. "Uh-oh," Ben whispered. "Things aren't going so good."

Assessment Connection

As you look over students' writing, keep anecdotal records about significant grammar and usage errors. If a number of students consistently make a common error, such as tense inconsistency or subject-verb agreement, reteach the concept in a small group setting.

Lesson Background

"What I know about grammar is its infinite power," states writer Joan Didion. Part of your job as a writing teacher is to help students appreciate the importance of correct grammar and usage in communicating their message clearly. This mini-lesson helps students understand the power of grammar and usage as tools that help them use the written word effectively.

Teaching the Lesson

Author C. S. Lewis says, "Always write . . . with the ear. . . . You should hear every sentence you write as if it was being read aloud or spoken." Reading your writing aloud is one way to check whether it sounds correct.

Display the overhead transparency and read it aloud.

What did you notice as you listened to this paragraph? *(Parts do not sound right.)* What are your impressions of the writer? *(Writer did not take time to polish it; writer does not sound like an experienced writer; writer does not take pride in the writing.)*

People form impressions about you from your writing just as they do from your behavior. What impressions do you want to make with your writing? *Accept students' responses.*

Look again at the passage about Luis and Ben. What errors in grammar and usage can you spot? *Have volunteers use proofreading symbols to mark the errors. Then have volunteers make corrections to the transparency. Errors include subject-verb agreement, wrong tense, and confusion in usage of* herd/heard *and* good/well.

Now look at a piece of writing you are ready to revise. Use proofreading symbols to mark any errors in grammar and usage.

Practicing the Skill

- Have students correct errors in grammar and usage in their marked drafts. When they are finished, ask them to exchange their drafts with a partner. Have partners read each other's work to double-check that all errors were found and corrected.

- Remind students to refer to the *Writer's Handbook* or another writer's reference book as they check their writing for correct grammar and usage. If students have individual copies of these books, suggest that they use sticky notes to mark sections they refer to often.

Checking Capitalization

Lesson Background

The poet e.e. cummings made an art form of ignoring capitalization rules. Most writers, however, use standard capitalization in order to communicate clearly. This mini-lesson reviews the capitalization rules your students have been studying since the primary grades.

Teaching the Lesson

You have studied the rules of capitalization for as long as you have been writing. It is easy to forget them, though, when you are concentrating on getting your ideas on paper. Let's review these rules. *Have students identify some of the rules of capitalization, such as using capital letters at the beginnings of sentences, for proper nouns, for book titles, for dates, and so on. List the rules on chart paper. You may want to refer to pages 4–7 in the* Writer's Handbook. *Display the completed chart where students can easily see it.*

Display the passage you wrote on chart paper. Think about the rules of capitalization we just discussed. What capitalization errors can you find in this passage? *Mark the errors students identify, using the appropriate proofreading symbol.*

Now choose a piece of writing you are revising and proofread it for errors in capitalization. Use the correct proofreading symbols to mark any changes that are needed. You can use the chart we created today as a capitalization checklist.

Practicing the Skill

- Provide students with real-life opportunities to use capitalization skills, such as creating a class list of names and addresses, writing and addressing letters, or creating a list of specific people or businesses and institutions to contact about a school project.

- Encourage students to develop the habit of making one proofreading pass through their writing in which they look only for capitalization errors.

You Will Need

- chart paper
- markers
- the following text written on chart paper:

Leah and Marcus got on the train in New York city. This was the first time they were going to visit grandpa in Washington, d.c. he was going to take them to the Smithsonian museum. Then they would have lunch at a spanish restaurant.

Assessment Connection

Before assessing a student's writing, scan for errors in capitalizing sentence beginnings, proper nouns, and adjectives. Ask students to correct these errors before you continue assessing their work. Note other capitalization errors and refer students who are having difficulty to the appropriate rules on pages 4–7 of the *Writer's Handbook* or another similar resource. If a number of students make frequent errors with a more difficult concept, such as words used as names, consider reteaching the rule in a small group setting.

Checking Punctuation

Lesson Background

"Anyone who can improve a sentence of mine by the omission or placing of a comma is . . . my best friend," says author George Moore. Because they understand how it affects flow and meaning, experienced authors respect the power of punctuation. This mini-lesson reminds students of the importance of checking their completed writing for correct punctuation.

Teaching the Lesson

1. Ask students why punctuation is important to writers. Record their responses on the chalkboard or on chart paper. Then display the sentences you wrote on chart paper. Ask students to read the first pair of sentences silently. Have a volunteer point out the punctuation mark that was added in the second sentence (hyphen). Review the function of the punctuation as it is used in the sentence (creating an adjective that modifies the noun *fish*). Discuss how the added punctuation changes the meaning.

2. Continue in the same way with the other sentence pairs. Remind students that just as the added punctuation changes the meaning of each sentence, misplaced or misused punctuation can cause confusion for their readers.

3. Review common punctuation marks and their functions. You may want to refer to pages 8–15 of the *Writer's Handbook*.

4. Have students select a piece of writing that is ready for proofreading. Ask them to go through their writing, concentrating only on punctuation. Remind them to use proofreading symbols to mark any errors they find. Then have them exchange their writing with a partner and check each other's work.

Practicing the Skill

Let students work with partners to create pairs of sentences similar to the samples you presented on chart paper. Remind them that the sentences should be the same except for punctuation, and that both versions must make sense. Have them record their sentence pairs and display them in the classroom for other students to read and analyze.

Checking Spelling

Lesson Background

Students are often told not to worry about spelling at the draft stage. However, standard spelling is key to clear communication in finished writing. This mini-lesson provides students with several tools for checking spelling.

Teaching the Lesson

1. Ask students to share their techniques for checking spelling in their writing. List their ideas on chart paper. Then display the text you wrote, masking all but the first sentence. Say, "One idea you suggested was rereading to find common spelling errors. Who can do that in this sentence?" Have students find and correct the errors (*could't* and *believe*).

2. Reveal the second sentence. Say, "Another technique is to use the dictionary to check spelling. This is especially valuable when we use unusual words in our writing. What words in this sentence should probably be looked up?" (*filospher* and *hummanatarian*) Comment that it may seem difficult to use the dictionary when you don't know how to spell a word. However, thinking about different ways to spell sounds and common root words can help. Help students understand that when *filospher* cannot be found under *f,* they can try *ph.* And remembering the spelling of the root word *human* will take them to the correct spelling of *humanitarian.*

3. Have students read the last sentence and point out words that may be misspelled (*all ready* and *stationary*). Remind them that words used incorrectly are considered misspellings. Discuss the correct words to use in the sentence.

4. Ask students to choose a piece of their own writing that is at the revision stage, and have them proofread it for spelling errors. Remind them to use some of the techniques they have discussed in this mini-lesson.

Practicing the Skill

- Encourage students to keep a spelling log of words they commonly misspell or misuse. Have them refer to the log when they use these words in their writing.

- When students begin a new piece of writing, suggest that they make a lightly penciled question mark next to words whose spelling they want to check. When they are finished writing, they can go back and look for the marked words in their spelling logs or the dictionary.

You Will Need

- chart paper
- markers
- the following text written on chart paper:

Ned could't beleive that it was time to go.

The filospher received a hummanatarian award.

Did you all ready use the whole box of stationary?

Teacher Tip

Create a chart or bulletin board with the heading "Tricky Spelling Words" and post on it words that a number of students regularly misspell. Refer students to the list when they are revising their writing.

Assessment Connection

Occasionally check students' drafts during the revision stage for evidence that spelling errors are being noted. If some students appear to be skipping this stage of revision, work with them individually. Put a question mark next to misspelled words, asking questions such as, "Does this word look right to you?" "What is the root word of this word?" or "Did you check this spelling in the dictionary?"

Criteria for Publishing

Lesson Background

Students often write merely for the learning experience or for their own satisfaction. However, there are ample opportunities for them to share their work with a wider audience by publishing it. Completing a piece of writing through the publication stage reinforces the idea that the purpose of writing is communication. This mini-lesson helps students determine when their writing is ready for publication.

Teaching the Lesson

1. Discuss with students what it means to publish a piece of writing (to make it available in some form for an audience of readers). Have students brainstorm a list of qualities that they think writing should have in order to be considered ready for publication. List their ideas on chart paper. Student responses may include: writing that is suitable for its audience; engages the reader; is free of errors in spelling, punctuation, and grammar; is legible; and so on.

2. Point out that there are many opportunities for students to publish their work. But before doing so, they must prepare the writing for publication. This means evaluating a piece of writing to see that it meets certain standards. Explain that the chart created in the previous activity can be used as a checklist of publishing standards.

3. Explain that, in addition to being sure their writing meets certain standards, professional writers create Publishing Proposals that are written to a person or company that may consider publishing the work. In it, the author answers questions such as:

   - What is the purpose of this piece?
   - Who is the intended audience?
   - Why would they be interested in reading the work?
   - How is this piece different from other writing on the same topic?

4. Ask students to meet in pairs to review each other's portfolios and identify writing that could be prepared for publication.

Practicing the Skill

- Display the checklist of publishing standards. Have students use it to make final preparations for publishing the pieces they have selected.

- Ask students to select one piece of writing and prepare a Publishing Proposal that answers the questions identified in this mini-lesson.

You Will Need

- chart paper
- markers

Teacher Tip

Reinforce the idea that writing that is published should be error-free. Have students carefully proofread final copies of writing they have selected for publication. Then have them share their final copies with a classmate who will proofread their work.

Assessment Connection

Conduct individual conferences with students to assess their Publishing Proposals and the writing they have prepared for publication. If there are areas in which you feel the student can improve, ask specific questions such as, "Did you check that each line of dialogue begins with a new paragraph?" or "Why would readers be interested in this piece of writing?"

Real-Life Publishing

Lesson Background

Your students have published their writing by sharing it in classroom and school settings. However, most of them have probably not experienced the thrill of publishing for a broader audience. In this mini-lesson, students submit writing to a person, institution, or publisher in the community or beyond.

Teaching the Lesson

1. Tell students that they will have a chance to publish their writing outside of the school. Point out that authors usually use agents to help them find places to publish their writing. Explain that you will act as their agent.

2. List on chart paper the publishing options you have identified from the suggestions in the Teacher Tip. Ask students to add suggestions as well. Explain any specific requirements for different options, such as sending a self-addressed, stamped envelope. Be sure that students understand the slow response time and possibilities of rejection faced when sending work to commercial publishers. However, try not to discourage them from doing so. You may want to point out that even the best-known authors often have trouble getting published commercially. For example, Madeleine L'Engle's book *A Wrinkle in Time* was rejected by many publishers before finally being published.

3. Ask students to reread their finished writing and Publishing Proposals from Mini-lesson 60. Have them review the list of publishing options and decide where to submit their work. Then explain that writers send cover letters to introduce themselves and their work to potential publishers. Have students draft cover letters to accompany the work they are submitting. When students have completed their letters, supervise the mailing or delivery of their work to the appropriate places and remind them to keep a copy of what they're submitting.

Practicing the Skill

- Set up procedures for students to submit work that they feel is ready for publication. Encourage students to consider outside publication several times during the school year.

- Establish a class Web site as one avenue for publishing students' writing. Have students select pen names to use for Internet publishing. Be sure to caution students against revealing personal information on the Web site.

You Will Need

- chart paper
- markers
- suggestions for publication options (see Teacher Tip)
- students' prepared writing and Publishing Proposals from Mini-lesson 60

Teacher Tip

Before teaching this mini-lesson, investigate possibilities for publishing student work. Consider the following:
- public library display of student writing
- picture books and stories for a pediatrician's waiting room
- historical society display of work related to the institution's theme
- display in a local mall or place of business

Assessment Connection

Conduct "agent-writer" conferences with individual students to discuss their plans for publishing their work. If some students appear to have unrealistic expectations for publication, suggest that they consider another avenue or do multiple submissions—for example, sending their work to a children's magazine and for display at the public library.

Choosing a Title

Lesson Background

Comedian and author Fred Allen pointed out that an author couldn't publish a book without a title because people would not know how to ask for it. Titles identify books, but they also provide clues to content, purpose, and tone. In this mini-lesson, students consider techniques for choosing appropriate titles for their own writing.

Teaching the Lesson

I am writing a short story about a boy named Casey who goes to an odd computer camp for the summer. While he is there, many funny things happen to him. Right now, I am thinking about a title. I know that the title should give readers a clue as to what my story is about and make them want to read it. I also know that the title should match the content, purpose, and tone of my writing. So I made this chart to help me think about the story and a title for it. *Display the "Content/Purpose/Tone" chart you prepared and have students read it.*

These are the titles I have thought of so far. *Display the chart of title suggestions. Invite students to suggest other ideas for titles. Have the class discuss the list and make suggestions about which title might work best and why. Remind them to think about the content, purpose, and tone of the story as they suggest and evaluate titles.*

I know I can always change the title when I'm finished writing. I can use just a "working title" for now.

Have students look through their portfolios to find examples of untitled writing. Ask them each to make a "Content/Purpose/Tone" chart for one piece of their writing. Then have them brainstorm some title ideas.

Practicing the Skill

- Have students work with partners to review their "Content/Purpose/Tone" charts and get input about which title best fits the selected piece of writing. Ask students to add the selected title to their writing draft.

- Share this quotation by Robert Penn Warren: "Sometimes people give titles to me, and sometimes I see them on a billboard." Discuss what Warren means by these words. Then have students review their portfolios and explain to a partner their inspiration for the title of one piece.

You Will Need

- markers
- the following text written on chart paper:

Content: boy who goes away to a summer computer camp

Purpose: to entertain

Tone: funny

- the following text written on a second sheet of chart paper:

Computer Summer Camp

Computer Camp Catastrophes

All You Need to Know About Computer Camp

Mosquito Bytes

Casey Goes Camping

Assessment Connection

When conferencing about a piece of writing, have students share with you the "Content/Purpose/Tone" charts they created to help them title the work. Evaluate whether the title reflects the information on the chart. Discuss title choices with students, asking questions such as "What made you choose this title?" or "What clues do you think this title gives readers about the content, purpose, or tone of your writing?"

Self-Assessment

Lesson Background

Experienced writers are accustomed to having their work critiqued by outsiders. But they also understand that to grow in their craft, they must evaluate their work according to their own standards as well. In this mini-lesson, students learn the value of reflecting on their own writing and how to use this reflection for self-assessment.

Teaching the Lesson

After a game or competition, athletes sometimes replay videotapes of themselves in action. They look for what they did well and where they might need to improve their skills. Writers evaluate their past performances in the same way—they look at their completed writing to reflect on what they like about it and what they want to work on. For example, when I recently looked at a story I wrote, I thought about what I liked and what I wanted to try to do better the next time I wrote a similar piece. Now I am going to make a chart to help me remember my reflections. *Display the overhead transparency of BLM 63. Record the title of the piece and the genre. Then reflect aloud and record what you were most proud of, what you would like to improve, and a technique you might use to do so. For example, if your goal is to create more vivid characters in a short story, you might decide to use a Character Traits Web organizer as a prewriting activity for your next story. Provide each student with a copy of the Self-Assessment Chart.*

Now, revisit a piece of writing you have completed recently. Look at what you wrote, and think about the processes you used. Reflect on what you feel you did well and what you would like to improve in your next piece of writing. Then record your ideas on the Self-Assessment Chart so that you can refer to it the next time you write a similar piece.

Practicing the Skill

- Have students store their charts in folders. Occasionally, ask them to complete Self-Assessment Charts for other pieces of writing and add these to their folders as well. Encourage students to review relevant charts before they begin a new piece in a particular genre.

- Introduce students to other self-assessment tools, such as rating scales and rubrics. You may want to develop a class scale or rubric that can be reproduced for students to use when assessing their writing.

You Will Need

- sample of your own writing
- overhead projector
- transparency markers
- overhead transparency of BLM 63 (Self-Assessment Chart)
- photocopies of BLM 63 for students

Assessment Connection

When you meet with students for assessment conferences, have them bring their folders of Self-Assessment Charts. Together, review any charts that relate to the piece of writing being assessed. Ask the student to explain how he or she used the chart when writing the piece. If it appears that a student did not follow through on goals and suggestions on the chart, discuss ways he or she might do so and how these suggestions might influence revisions.

Writing Logs: Analyzing Your Writing

You Will Need

- marker
- recent writing samples
- BLM 64 copied onto chart paper (Writing Log Assessment Chart)
- photocopies of BLM 64 for each student

Revising Tip

Point out to students that referring back to their writing logs often can help them recall skills and techniques they have mastered and may want to apply to a piece of writing they are currently revising.

Assessment Connection

Meet with students on a monthly basis to review their writing logs. As you go through their portfolios, ask them questions to assess how realistic they have been in identifying strengths—for example, "How does this example show that your characters are well developed?" Also discuss students' goals and look at subsequent writing to discuss whether those goals are being met.

Lesson Background

In addition to self-assessing individual pieces of writing, students benefit from taking wide-angle views of their writing over time. Tracking their progress helps students feel a sense of accomplishment and provides incentive for future growth.

Teaching the Lesson

1. Ask students who have younger siblings, cousins, or neighbors to share signs of growth they have seen in these children (for example, progressing from crawling to walking). Comment that these growth spurts are easy to see, and that many families keep track of them with photographs or videotapes.

2. Point out that writers also grow, but that this kind of change is harder to notice and record. Suggest that a writing log is one way to chart their growth in writing. Explain that students will be completing individual writing logs at the end of each month. In these logs, they will revisit the writing they did over the course of the month to assess and summarize the skills they have mastered.

3. Display the Writing Log Assessment Chart. Record your own name and identify the month during which the log is being kept. In the *My Strengths* section, list three or four traits or skills shown in your writing samples; for example: *careful nonfiction research, strong dialogue, selection of vivid verbs.* In the *Writing Examples* section, record the title of a piece of writing or a word or phrase from your writing samples. As you complete the log, reflect aloud about how you identified the strengths in your writing and why you think your examples exemplify those traits. Then list two or three writing goals you would like to work toward in the coming month.

4. Distribute copies of the Writing Log Assessment Chart to students, and have them revisit writing they have created in the last month. Stress that the traits identified as strengths are the areas of their writing in which they feel they are doing well. Areas of their writing that they feel need improvement should be listed as goals.

Practicing the Skill

One month from now, have students create another writing log based on that month's writing. Have them revisit their writing goals from the previous month and assess their progress in reaching those goals.

Writing Strategy Cards for Grade 5

The *Wonder Writers* Writing Strategy Cards offer a unique blend of writing instruction. The attractive, engaging posters focus on both the essentials of writing: rules for grammar, usage, and mechanics as well as identifying how successful writers think! The Writing Strategy Cards help students understand how language acquisition connects to our experiences and connects us to the world. The Writing Strategy Cards take students to the next level in their writing by having them ask, "What do other writers do? What can I do?" The 32 cards (16 two-sided cards) at the Grade 5 level serve as a resource for the students and for you. They highlight real-world connections to specific strategies used by all writers, regardless of experience or expertise.

A Teacher Page and a Student Activity Page accompany each card. In the left-hand column of the teacher page you will find a box labeled *Teacher Tip.* The Teacher Tip provides you with an introduction to the Student Activity Page.

While the Student Activity Pages are designed to be supplemental, independent, extension activities, a brief introduction to the page is recommended. This will ensure that your expectations are clear and allow students an opportunity to have their questions answered before they engage in independent practice. Also, in listening to students' questions and areas of concern, you will be able to anticipate those students who may need some additional small group instruction to strengthen their understanding.

The Teacher Tip provides you with a summary of the lesson, revisiting the key points that you will want to highlight with your students. If there are any additional materials needed for the lesson, a list of suggested items may appear in the box as well.

Often the Writing Strategy Cards include trade titles that give specific examples of what is being portrayed in the lesson and suggest ways in which to present the book to the students. In the *Literature Connection* box you will find titles from that particular page that you might want to include as a reference in your lesson.

You may choose to select specific lessons as needed or you may want to follow the suggested teaching order as outlined on the following pages. The suggested teaching order simply reflects the organization of the Writing Strategy Cards. If you choose to match the cards more closely to the guidelines of your curriculum or the areas of development for your students, you are in no way inhibiting the integrity of the program. The Writing Strategy Cards were created for ease and flexibility within your curriculum as well as being able to meet the individual needs of your students.

Suggested Teaching Order for Writing Strategy Cards Grade 5

Writing Strategy Cards:
1—Writers solve problems.
17—Writers write about people.

Writing Strategy Cards:
2—Writers explain.
18—Writers wonder.

Writing Strategy Cards:
3—Writers remember the past.
19—Writers write about special moments.

Writing Strategy Cards:
4—Writers experiment.
20—Writers notice little things.

Writing Strategy Cards:
5—Writers are people-watchers and good listeners.
21—Writers write about the unexpected and unusual.

Writing Strategy Cards:
6—Writers are poets.
22—Writers reread and rewrite.

Writing Strategy Cards:
7—Writers collect writing they like.
23—Writers write about things that are important to them.

Writing Strategy Cards:

8—Writers are curious.

24—Writers are all different.

Writing Strategy Cards:

9—Writers get to the point.

25—Writers collect ideas.

Writing Strategy Cards:

10—Writers write with a purpose.

26—Writers don't always start at the beginning.

Writing Strategy Cards:

11—Writers are readers.

27—Writers describe.

Writing Strategy Cards:

12—Writers persuade.

28—Writers daydream and imagine.

Writing Strategy Cards:

13—Writers aren't always inspired.

29—Writers get help.

Writing Strategy Cards:

14—Writers investigate and collect facts.

30—Writers write for their readers.

Writing Strategy Cards:

15—Writers are storytellers.

31—Writers are reporters.

Writing Strategy Cards:

16—Writers learn from other writers.

32—Writers send messages.

Writers solve problems.

People who write letters to the editor, employees who create action plans, and journalists who pen articles about environmental issues all use their skills to address problems and suggest solutions. These activities help students understand the power of the written word to provide solutions for the problems they face.

Making the Connection

- Ask students to identify the problem on the card. (The girl lost her dog.) Have a volunteer explain how writing helped to solve the problem. (Someone saw her sign and found and returned the dog.) Discuss other ways the girl could have solved her problem with writing, such as putting a notice in the Lost and Found section of the newspaper.

- Point out that writing can be used to help people think about and solve a variety of problems—personal, community, and global. Have students brainstorm types of writing that are often used for these purposes, such as writing journal entries to help you think through personal problems, petitions to address community issues, and essays or books to bring global problems to the attention of a worldwide audience.

Connecting to Real Life

- Have students identify several problems that exist in their school or community, such as inadequate school computer facilities or lack of community participation in recycling programs. Challenge them to brainstorm ways writing could be used to address these problems.

- Share nonfiction books that deal with solving problems. Ask students to surmise the problems addressed by reviewing titles, tables of contents, and headings. For example, discuss *The Kid's Guide to Social Action* by Barbara A. Lewis and *Worms Eat My Garbage: How to Set Up and Maintain a Worm Composting System* by Mary Appelhof and Mary F. Fenton.

Just for You

Think of a problem in education that matters deeply to you. Write notes about what you believe is the solution. Consider using your notes to write an article for submission to a professional journal, publication in a district-wide newsletter, or as a letter to the editor of the local newspaper.

Literature Connection

- *The Kid's Guide to Social Action* by Barbara A. Lewis
- *Worms Eat My Garbage: How to Set Up and Maintain a Worm Composting System* by Mary Appelhof and Mary F. Fenton

Teacher Tip

Writers often play an important role as problem-solvers. The following Student Activity Page guides students through the process of writing a draft that addresses a particular problem. Encourage students to revise their writing, illustrate as necessary, and share their work with the class.

Writers solve problems.

Don't complain about problems, solve them! But how? Throughout history, writers have relied on the written word to make the world a better place. You can, too.

Pick a Problem

Pick a problem that exists in your community, such as littering or the lack of new equipment in schools. Write to address the problem and offer a possible solution.

1. **Determine your audience by deciding who could take action or bring the problem to the attention of others—a newspaper editor? a politician? your principal?**
2. **Choose the format best suited for your topic and audience. For example, you could write a letter or a report or design a brochure or a poster.**
3. **Write about the problem and solution. Include the following:**
   - **a topic sentence that explains the problem and grabs the reader's attention**
   - **a description of a possible solution, including the steps to be taken, people involved, and resources needed**
   - **a conclusion that summarizes your solution and a possible action that the reader can follow**

Help Yourself

Writing can help with frustrating problems you might have in your daily life. Create a problems-solutions chart that you can use.

1. **Think of a personal problem that you don't mind sharing. Maybe you and a friend aren't getting along, or you don't want to share a room with your little brother. At the top of a sheet of paper, write a clear explanation of the problem.**
2. **Think of several possible solutions to the problem.**
3. **Draw a large box for each solution. Label your solution boxes, and write a sentence that describes the solution. Under the sentence, list the good and bad points of each solution.**

Writers explain.

Literature Connection

- *Kids Around the World Cook! The Best Foods and Recipes from Many Lands* by Arlette Braman
- *You Asked? Over 300 Great Questions and Astounding Answers* edited by Katherine Farris
- *Earth Book for Kids: Activities to Help Heal the Environment* by Linda Schwartz

Teacher Tip

On the following Student Activity Page students are given an opportunity to practice writing clear, organized explanations.

If you feel that much of the writing you do is explanatory, you are not alone. For most people, explanatory writing makes up the bulk of their writing efforts. Equipping students with explanatory writing skills will prepare them for the day-to-day writing most of them do now and will do as adults.

Making the Connection

- Have students discuss what the children shown on the card are doing (reading the explanation of a museum display). Ask how the writer of the explanation might have gotten the information he or she needed (research, interviews, and so on).

- Challenge students to think of other forms of explanatory writing. Generate a class list of examples, such as textbooks, how-to books, instruction manuals, cookbooks, and game directions.

Connecting to Real Life

- Point out that writers use different techniques for explanatory writing. Share some of these techniques and examples of each: procedural writing (*Kids Around the World Cook! The Best Foods and Recipes from Many Lands* by Arlette Braman); question and answer (*You Asked? Over 300 Great Questions and Astounding Answers* edited by Katherine Farris); compare and contrast (use textbook examples); and problem and solution (*Earth Book for Kids: Activities to Help Heal the Environment* by Linda Schwartz). Ask students to identify characteristics of each type of writing, such as materials lists or numbered steps.

- Share samples of your own explanatory writing with the class, such as homework instructions or a letter to the editor. Discuss strategies you used to explain your thoughts and ideas.

- Ask students to participate in an explanatory writing scavenger hunt. Over the course of a school day, have them note and record at least a dozen examples of explanatory writing they encounter. Have students share what they discovered.

Just for You

Think of something that mystifies and interests you. You might wonder how a particular machine or technology works or what the circumstances behind a historical event were. Find a book about that topic. Note the techniques the author uses to explain concepts. Consider using the same techniques to write a summary of what you learn.

Writers explain.

Do you sometimes get tongue-tied when trying to explain something? Explaining things in writing can be even more challenging. The secret to clear explanations is to predict the questions your readers will have and answer them in a clear and organized way.

Explain That!

People who set up museums know that visitors have questions about the displays. They try to answer these questions by posting explanations. Think about things in your school that visitors might question. Then write explanations that answer their questions.

1. **Identify things a visitor may need to have explained, such as the school name, policies for visitors, or computer facilities.**
2. **List specific questions a visitor might have. For example, "Why is the school named Byrd School?" and "Has it always had the same name?"**
3. **Write an explanation that answers the questions you identified. Make a final copy on sturdy paper and display it near what is being explained or on a bulletin board titled "About Our School."**

A How-To Booklet

Share what you know by writing a how-to booklet.

1. **Think about something you know how to do or make—such as a sport, craft, recipe, or game.**
2. **Mentally review what someone needs to know in order to do the activity or make the object. Think about the materials needed and the order of the steps.**
3. **Write a step-by-step explanation of the procedure.**
4. **Exchange your writing with a partner. Read each other's explanations to see if revisions are needed to make your explanation clear and understandable.**
5. **Compile final copies in a class binder titled "Fun Things We Know How to Do."**

Writers remember the past.

Writers remember and preserve stories from the past by writing in many formats, such as poetry, fiction, plays, biography, autobiography, and essays. Writers write about their own memories from the past— as well as about the memories of others. Writers use different ways to show time and the order of events when they write about the past.

Making the Connection

- Encourage students to discuss the illustration on the card. Students should infer that the girl is thinking and writing about an event from the past. In fact, she is probably writing about an actual historical event: Washington and his troops crossing the Delaware River during the Revolutionary War. Ask, "What kind of writing might the girl's research lead to?"

- Point out to students that many writers use historical research to help them write about the past, but there are other ways to learn and write about the past, too. Ask students to think about their own memories, and about stories they have heard from older relatives and friends. Together, discuss how these kinds of memories can be used by writers to write about the past.

Connecting to Real Life

- Explain that writers can "play" with time in creative ways as they write about the past. For example, introduce three books by Cynthia Rylant that order time in three different ways. In *Birthday Presents,* Rylant presents the events of the story in chronological order, each birthday following the one before it. In *When I Was Young in the Mountains,* the events of the story are presented as a series of "snapshots" from the past with no real linear sequence. And Rylant's novel *A Fine White Dust* opens briefly in the present, with the bulk of the book told as a flashback.

- Share a journal entry or orally share a memory from your own past. For example, tell about something that happened to you in fifth grade. Then discuss with students how you might approach writing about the experience.

Just for You

Choose one of your own family stories and make some notes about the sequence of events. Then write two or more versions of the story, experimenting with time order. Consider using flashbacks or snapshots, and/or slowing and speeding time.

Literature Connection

- *Birthday Presents* by Cynthia Rylant
- *When I Was Young in the Mountains* by Cynthia Rylant
- *A Fine White Dust* by Cynthia Rylant
- *The Cabin Faced West* by Jean Fritz
- *Pauses: Autobiographical Reflections of 101 Creators of Children's Books* by Lee Bennett Hopkins

Teacher Tip

On the following Student Activity Page students are asked to write about family history and to write historical fiction. Explain that stories from the past can be in the form of poetry, fiction, plays, autobiographies, and essays. Discuss how writing about the past can be presented chronologically, in no real linear sequence, or as a flashback.

Writers remember the past.

Jean Fritz based her book *The Cabin Faced West* on the experiences of her pioneer great-great grandmother, Ann Hamilton. Fritz explains that while writing this historical book, she "discovered the joys of research. It was like exploring. Digging into American history also seemed to satisfy a need that I had. . . ." (*Pauses: Autobiographical Reflections of 101 Creators of Children's Books* by Lee Bennett Hopkins, Section 25)

Family History

Think about family stories you've heard from parents or grandparents. Do you know a story about how an ancestor came to this country, how your grandparents met, or how you kept your parents up every night when you were a newborn baby?

Choose a family story to write about. Choose a story you know well, but be creative in your writing. Instead of telling the story as a third-person narrator, imagine that you were a participant. Put yourself in the shoes of a parent or grandparent, and write the story from his or her point of view.

World History

Historical fiction is based on events from the past, but includes ideas from the writer's imagination as well.

Choose an event from the past that you have studied or read about. Then write a short story based on the event. Use some historical facts, and bring them to life by combining them with your own ideas and experiences. For example, although you couldn't have crossed the Delaware with Washington and his men, you might have experienced cold, hunger, exhaustion, or fear. Combine details like these with historical facts to make the past come alive in your writing.

Writers experiment.

Literature Connection

- *Help, I'm Trapped in an Alien's Body* by Todd Strasser
- *A Wrinkle in Time* by Madeleine L'Engle

Teacher Tip

Writers can keep their work interesting by using new styles and word choices. The following Student Activity Page encourages students to try new words in their writing and to write a piece in a writing style they do not usually use. Encourage students to share their completed work with the class.

School art programs encourage students to draw, paint, and sculpt many different subjects using varied media. The same is true of a vibrant writing program. Encourage students to step out of their "comfort zones," and entice them to experiment with words, topics, styles, and techniques.

Making the Connection

- Have students tell how the picture on the card depicts experimentation. Ask, "What ideas do the combinations of words on the card spark for you?" Initiate a discussion with students about the importance of reading and writing new things. Point out that when writers open their minds and experiment with language, they discover new ways to communicate.

- Ask students to list foods they have eaten in the past few days. Then direct them to list kinds of reading they have done in the past few months. Finally, have them identify kinds of writing they have done recently. Pose the question, "Does your food diet have more variety than your reading and writing diets do? Why?"

Connecting to Real Life

- Share Todd Strasser's words with students, "I originally wrote a lot of books for teens because that is where I had my first success and felt most confident. But as I grow older, I find my interests widening. . . . I'd like to think the day will come when I will write books for people of all ages, from three to eighty-three." Strasser has written many books for teens, as well as books for younger readers, such as *Help, I'm Trapped in an Alien's Body*. Ask students how they feel about Strasser's views and what they can learn from him.

- Not only has Madeleine L'Engle tried various kinds of writing, she has woven together more than one genre—science fiction and fantasy, for example—in books such as *A Wrinkle in Time*. Tell students that she advises, "Be open. . . . Be ready to change." Ask students to explain how they might follow this advice in their writing.

Just for You

Identify a type of writing that intimidates you. Perhaps your stomach clenches when you think about composing poetry. Maybe the idea of writing a news article gives you hives. Be brave. Try a different type of writing. You may find that the experience is both challenging and rewarding.

Writers experiment.

Do you wear the same exact outfit every day? Probably not! Just as you change your outfits, you need to vary what you read and write. Use these activities to avoid getting in a rut of reading the same types of books and writing about the same topics using the same style and vocabulary over and over again.

New Words

You can get stuck in the rut of overusing the same words. This makes your writing dull. Create a "word collection" that you can draw from, and experiment with new words.

1. **Create a chart in your writer's notebook using headings such as _Powerful Verbs_, _Specific Nouns_, and _Colorful Modifiers_.**
2. **When you read, note words that are interesting or unusual and add them to your chart.**
3. **Look through your portfolio to see if there are words you overuse, such as _said_. Use a dictionary and a thesaurus to look up alternatives for overused words; add the alternatives to your chart.**
4. **When you revise your writing, use these new words that you haven't used before.**

Try on a New Style

Do you tend to read mainly science fiction? biographies? fantasy? poems? news articles? Try reading a genre that is new to you. Then try writing a piece using that genre's style. Remember—this is an experiment—challenge yourself!

1. **Choose a story, an article, or a poem that is written in a style you do not normally read. Notice what makes the style special.**
2. **Choose a writing topic. As you write your own draft, refer to the piece you read.**
3. **After you have finished a first draft, think of ways you can change the style a bit to make it your own; then, revise it.**

Writers are people-watchers and good listeners.

Writers watch and listen to people to learn how they look and what they do and say. As Anne Lamott says, "Writing is about learning to pay attention" (*Bird by Bird,* Section 14). Observing and listening enable writers to create realistic characters for their writing.

Literature Connection

A Writer's Notebook: Unlocking the Writer Within You by Ralph Fletcher

Teacher Tip

Writers must carefully observe people around them in order to bring their characters to life. On the following Student Activity Page students are directed to observe a conversation and write it as a short dialogue. You might want to have students take the role of different speakers and read the dialogue aloud.

Making the Connection

- Invite students to discuss how the writing strategy is illustrated on the card. Help students to understand that the girl is carefully listening and watching as the mother sings to and interacts with her baby. The girl is making mental notes about what she sees and hears.

- Explain that including details of a person's appearance, words, actions, and gestures in their writing can bring a character to life. For example, describe to students a favorite relative, including that person's appearance and personality traits. Together, create a fictional character based on the details you provided.

Connecting to Real Life

- Share Ralph Fletcher's striking metaphor: "The goal of a writer is to be a sponge" (*A Writer's Notebook,* Chapter 5). Ask students what Fletcher means, and have them discuss how absorbing everything can help a writer.

- Write down a funny or unusual conversation you hear. Read it aloud to your students, and together discuss what the dialogue reveals about the speakers' characteristics.

- Ask each student to think about a vivid, memorable fictional character. Then have students identify and share specific details that bring the character to life by answering these questions: "How does the character look? What is unusual or unique about the character? How does the character speak?"

Just for You

The next time you are in a crowded supermarket or pharmacy, practice your people-watching and listening skills. Note the different ways people look, move, and speak. Use one of these "characters" in a piece of writing.

Writers are people-watchers and good listeners.

The writer Anne Lamott says, "I took notes on the people around me, in my town, in my family, in my memory . . . I wrote down funny stuff I overheard. I learned to be like a ship's rat, veined ears trembling, and I learned to scribble it all down" (*Bird by Bird*, Acknowledgments). You've probably never dreamed of being a ship's rat! But it can help your writing to act like one! Watch and listen intently to people all around you.

How Do They Look?

Write a paragraph that describes how a relative or a friend looks. Focus on one or two small but significant details that reveal a lot about the person's character. For example, you might write about your grandmother's deep wrinkles that appear to create smiling shapes on her face or your friend's sparkling green eyes.

What Do They Do?

Choose a different relative or friend to write about. Observe (or remember) his or her actions, movements, and gestures. Pay particular attention to:

- repeated gestures (such as nervously twisting his or her hair over and over);
- actions that seem to show what the person is like (such as feeding every stray cat that comes to town); and
- personality traits (such as a unique, contagious laugh).

What Do They Say?

Listen to the different ways people talk, noting *what* people say and *how* they say it. Jot down notes about a conversation that reveals some aspect of the speaker's character. Later, write a short dialogue based on the conversation.

Writers are poets.

Students are sometimes hesitant about writing poetry. By providing examples of many different poetic forms, you can help spark students' delight in poetry and show them that they can indeed express themselves poetically.

Making the Connection

- Cover the verse on the card, and then ask students to examine the picture. Have them brainstorm phrases a poet might use to describe the scene. Uncover the poem and have students read it.

- Discuss poetic forms that a writer could use, such as haiku, rhymed couplets, free verse, and so on. Review the characteristics of these poems and the concepts of rhythm and rhyme in poetry.

Connecting to Real Life

- Compose a class free-verse poem about snowboarding or another experience common to students. Create a web by writing the topic at the center of a sheet of chart paper and circling it. Add more circles around the center. In the circles, record phrases and ideas suggested by students. Encourage them to include sensory details. When the web is finished, have students review it. Let them organize the words and phrases on the web into a free-verse poem. Record the poem on another sheet of chart paper and provide time for students to suggest revisions.

- Point out that poetry is a very personal kind of writing. An infinite number of poems can be written on any topic—each reflecting the unique thoughts, impressions, and voice of its writer. Present an anthology of poems on one subject, such as *Marvelous Math: A Book of Poems* selected by Lee Bennett Hopkins. Share several examples, including rhymed poems and free verse.

Just for You

Let your mind wander its way into poetry. Think of a topic that evokes your emotions. Close your eyes and let your thoughts roam for a few minutes. Then open your eyes and start writing. Don't worry about using complete sentences—just capture as many of your ideas as possible. Organize your ideas into a free-verse format that sounds right to you.

Writers are poets.

What came before novels, short stories, and plays? Poetry! Poetry is one of the oldest forms of literature. For thousands of years, people have used poems to express feelings and relate their views about the world.

Rhyme Time

Think of a happy event you experienced recently, such as a surprise party or a family barbecue. Now write a rhyming poem about the event.

1. **Get your ideas down in short lines. Do not worry about rhyming yet.**
2. **Look at books of poetry to see rhyming patterns other poets have used, such as four-line verses in which the ends of the first and third lines rhyme and the second and fourth lines rhyme (ABAB). Choose one pattern to use as a model or create your own rhyming scheme.**
3. **Revise your poem so that it rhymes. You can change words, rearrange the order of words or lines, and so on.**
4. **Use a tape recorder to record yourself reading your poem aloud. Listen to the recording to hear how the rhyme pattern sounds.**

Follow a Pattern

Some poems follow specific patterns. Choose one of the following unrhymed patterns and write a poem to fit that format.

Quinzaine	Cinquain
Line 1: Statement of 7 syllables	Line 1: 2 syllables (subject of the poem)
The sun peers through the droplets.	**Water**
Line 2: Begin question with 5 syllables	Line 2: 4 syllables (words that describe the subject)
Will a rainbow show	**Cool, wet, icy—**
Line 3: End question with 3 syllables	Line 3: 6 syllables (verbs that relate to the subject)
Its colors?	**Spurting, squirting, bubbling,**
	Line 4: 8 syllables (feelings about the subject)
	Satisfying my thirst again—
	Line 5: 2 syllables (synonym for the subject)
	Fountain.

Writers collect writing they like.

Writers love the printed word, and they are always on the lookout for good writing. Writers often go back and reread a favorite story, article, or poem. Writers know that each rereading of a favorite piece can uncover a new insight as well as provide inspiration for their own writing.

Making the Connection

- Ask students to look at the card and make some inferences about the owner of the locker in the picture. Students' responses should reveal that the locker's owner loves to play and watch sports, has an older brother, admires one professional athlete enough to correspond with him, saves letters and cards from people he cares about, and writes or collects poetry with special meaning.

- Tell students that each writer's collection of favorite writings is unique and personal. Ask students to surmise why the locker's owner saved the different pieces of writing on display. What different types of writing are represented?

Connecting to Real Life

- Bring in a wide selection of writings you love, such as favorite books from your own library, articles or clippings you have collected, comics posted on your refrigerator, or a poem you keep by your bedside. Give students some history and background for each special piece of writing; let your fondness for each piece show.

- Have students interview an adult to learn about treasured writings he or she has collected. Help students prepare for the interview by having them brainstorm questions they want to ask.

- Ask student volunteers to create a bulletin board of poetry and other short pieces. Help students think about how each piece might influence their own writing.

Just for You

An especially nice way to "collect" writing you like is to commit it to memory. Try memorizing a favorite poem. Don't attempt to memorize it all in one sitting; post it in a prominent place at home and at school, and carry a copy around with you so you can refer to it often.

Writers collect writing they like.

What's your favorite story? Is it a spooky one? a sad tale that brings tears to your eyes? a fantasy or adventure? Or do you love nonfiction—maybe life in ancient Egypt? Writers collect writing they love, and they reread favorite pieces often for inspiration and for pleasure.

Surprise! You Have a Library!

What's a library? It's a carefully chosen collection of writing. It may be large or small, public or private. Writers have libraries of their favorite writing, and you probably do, too.

On this list, check off the kinds of writing you have collected. Circle any that you would like to add to your personal library.

__ **Fiction**
  __ Fantasy
  __ Historical fiction
  __ Mystery
  __ Science fiction
  __ Realistic fiction
  __ Short stories
__ **Traditional literature**
  __ Fairy tales or folktales

__ Myths and legends
__ Fables
__ **Poetry**
__ **Plays**
__ **Letters**
__ **Nonfiction**
  __ Informational books
  __ Biographies or autobiographies

__ Magazine articles
__ Newspaper articles
__ **Reference books**
  __ Dictionary
  __ Atlas
  __ Encyclopedia
  __ Almanac
__ **Song lyrics**
__ **Jokes or comics**
__ **Other**

Think About It

Choose a piece of writing you really like.

1. **Think about the writing you have chosen. Reread it, or parts of it. What makes the writing special? a great beginning? realistic characters? In your writer's notebook, write a paragraph that explains what it is about the writing that makes it special for you.**
2. **You've just identified one or more ingredients of good writing. Now write a second paragraph. Discuss how you might use what you learned in your own writing.**

Writers are curious.

Writers are curious about the world around them. To satisfy their curiosity, writers observe, read, and listen to things they encounter in their daily lives. They make notes about what they learn and use those ideas in their writing.

Literature Connection

- *The Watsons Go to Birmingham, 1963* by Christopher Paul Curtis
- *Game Day: Behind the Scenes at a Ballpark* by Robert Young

Teacher Tip

Writers need to be curious and interested in the world around them. The following Student Activity Page helps spark students' curiosity by guiding them through a modified KWL chart that will help them create the setting of a fictional story or poem. Additionally, students will be given an opportunity to write a nonfiction article about a person who interests them. You may want to invite guests into the classroom who might serve as subjects of students' articles. Encourage students to be curious and to think of questions to ask the guests.

Making the Connection

- Ask students to describe what the girl pictured on the card is doing. Explain that writers are curious about people, places, and things around them. Ask students why they think curiosity is an important trait of good writers.

- Have students brainstorm ways to collect information about topics that spark their curiosity. List their suggestions on chart paper. Students should mention reading books and newspapers, talking to experts, watching videos, using the Internet, and so on.

Connecting to Real Life

- Talk about Christopher Paul Curtis, whose first novel, *The Watsons Go to Birmingham, 1963,* grew out of his curiosity about his parents and the Civil Rights movement. Curtis learned what he needed to know for his story by reading books and by talking to people who lived during that time period. Ask students to think about aspects of their family or community history that make them curious and how they would go about satisfying their curiosity.

- Have students make a curiosity web. Ask them to write *Curious about . . .* in the center of the web. Have them label the branches *People, Places,* and *Things.* Tell students to jot down on the branches topics that make them curious.

- Explain that Robert Young's curiosity led him to write many books. For example, when he was watching a baseball game, he wondered what happens behind the scenes in preparation for a game. He did research and used what he learned to write *Game Day: Behind the Scenes at a Ballpark.* Have students brainstorm behind-the-scenes situations that intrigue them.

Just for You

A writer asks questions, and the answers become stories. For one day, carry a small notebook with you. As you go through your day, jot down notes about some of the people, places, and things that arouse your curiosity. At the end of the day, review your notes and select an idea that could blossom into a story, poem, or essay.

Name _____ Date _____

Writers are curious.

If you could ask anybody anything, who and what would you ask? When you are curious about something, try to find the answers. All you need to do is know where to look, what to read, and whom to ask.

Curious People

People are often curious about others whose skills, interests, and ideas are different from their own. Write a nonfiction article about a person who interests you.

1. **Think of someone who sparks your curiosity. Write several questions you want to ask about that person.**
2. **If possible, interview the person, or use the Internet, newspapers, and reference books to answer your questions.**
3. **Draft an article about the person. Include interesting facts and quotations.**
4. **Publish the articles in a class newsletter titled "Curious People."**

A Curious Setting

Use your curiosity to create the setting of a fictional story or poem.

1. **Think of a place that makes you curious. Make three columns on a piece of paper. Title the columns *Know*, *Wonder*, and *Learn*. Write things you already know about the place under *Know*.**
2. **List things you would like to know about the place under *Wonder*.**
3. **With the help of your teacher or a media specialist, locate travel books, videos, and Internet sites to help you discover the answers to your *Wonder* questions. Write the answers under *Learn*.**
4. **Draft a story or poem using the place as a setting. Include facts from your chart and create characters who would be likely to live in this place.**
5. **Revise your story, and then share it with your classmates.**

Writers get to the point.

It takes practice and discipline to keep a piece of writing focused and on track. Writers get to the point—and stick to it—with careful planning and thoughtful revisions.

Making the Connection

- Ask students to look at the illustration on the card and think about how it reflects the strategy. Help students understand that the visual pun has a deeper meaning: that writers must work to focus, get to the point of their story, and continue to stay on track.

- Help students explore the differences between conversation and writing. Create a chart like the one below. Add student responses to the chart.

Conversation	Writing
can jump from topic to topic	focused on one topic
often includes extra words or expressions (*umm, you know*)	excludes extra, meaningless, or repetitive words
can rely on facial expressions and gestures to aid listener's understanding	written words must be clear enough to convey meaning; must not mislead

Connecting to Real Life

- Many writers find it difficult or too restrictive to preplan their writing in great detail. Share Ralph Fletcher's technique for making what he calls an *informal outline* to "chunk" ideas before writing. A very simple outline, he says, "creates four empty 'drawers,'" which help to "separate ideas and organize my thinking . . . [and] my writing" (*How Writers Work,* Chapter 3). Fletcher shows how a report on rain forests can be divided into four such categories: (1) Introduction, (2) Benefits of Rain Forests, (3) Destruction of Rain Forests, and (4) Conclusion. Explain that many types of outlines can help a writer stay on track.

- Share Fletcher's analogy between raspberry bushes—which grow back stronger after pruning—and writing: "You need to prune your writing, too. As you reread your writing, look at your words with a cold eye. What passages are extra, repetitive, or unnecessary? Where do you wander off the topic?" (*How Writers Work,* Chapter 9)

Just for You

Revisit an old draft of your writing. How can you better focus your writing? How can you make your point more effectively?

Literature Connection

How Writers Work: Finding a Process That Works for You by Ralph Fletcher

Teacher Tip

Much of the hard work involved in writing takes place before and after an author writes a draft. Writers need to plan and revise their work carefully. The following Student Activity Page provides students with questions they can consider in order to evaluate a piece of their writing, as well as tips for revising. To help students understand good revising techniques, you might want to write a paragraph on chart paper and then model revising it for the class.

Writers get to the point.

Get to the point! Get focused! Stay on track! You've probably heard this message hundreds of times. That's because it's good advice for all sorts of activities, including writing. Writers plan, and after drafting, they rewrite and revise to make sure their writing gets to the point—and sticks to it.

Pruning Time

Choose a draft that you have not worked on recently. Reread it with fresh eyes, and ask yourself questions such as these:

- Is any part of my writing repetitive or unnecessary?
- Do long descriptions slow down the action?
- Does my writing wander off the topic?
- Does each paragraph add something that helps make my meaning clearer?
- Does every sentence have a purpose? Does every word have a purpose?
- Is any important information missing?

Now, revise your writing and "get to the point."

Neat Tricks

Use these shortcuts to keep your work as neat (and readable) as possible when making changes to your drafts. You'll save time and cut down on the number of times you need to recopy your work during the revising process. (Of course, you'll still need to write a clean final copy.)

- **Write on every other line on all first drafts.**
- **Draw a single, neat line through words or sentences to be cut. Don't scribble things out.**
- **To insert a word or phrase, write it above the line. Then draw a pointer ∧ between the words where it should go.**
- **Draw a circle around sections you want to move. Then draw an arrow to the place they are moving.**
- **To start a new paragraph, insert this symbol: ¶ . Try using a different colored pencil for each round of revisions.**

Writers write with a purpose.

Teacher Tip

Writers write for a variety of reasons, and they must make sure their writing stays true to its intended purpose. The following Student Activity Page instructs students to choose a familiar topic and write five different paragraphs about it, each one for a different purpose. Encourage volunteers to read one of their paragraphs aloud, and invite students to guess what the purpose of the paragraph might be.

Writers write with a specific purpose in mind. Sometimes writers decide they want to entertain readers with a funny story. Other times, writers want to teach readers about a topic by providing factual information. It is important for writers to determine why they are writing before they decide exactly *what* they are going to write.

Making the Connection

- Have students look at the illustration on the card. Help them identify the porpoise on the card, and point out how the word *porpoise* sounds like *purpose*. Ask students what emotions are expressed on the faces of the writer and the audience. Encourage students to describe what they think might be the writer's purpose.

- Explain that all writing has a purpose, and it's important for writers to keep the purpose in mind as they write. Draw a web with the center oval labeled *Writing Purposes*. Draw five ovals branching off, labeled *request, inform, teach, persuade,* and *entertain*. Explain that almost everything students write falls into one of these categories. Ask students to identify and describe stories, articles, and other pieces of writing that they have read or written that fall into each category.

Connecting to Real Life

- Read a sample of writing that fits into each of the five categories in the web. After each reading, have students identify into which category it fits.

- Then have students ask themselves: "What will my reader learn or do after reading what I've written?" Ask students to think about the writing samples from the previous activity. What does the writer want readers to *do* or to *learn* after reading the piece?

- For more on writing with a purpose, refer to the following Writing Strategy Cards:

    2. Writers explain. (writing to teach)
    15. Writers are storytellers. (writing to entertain)
    31. Writers are reporters. (writing to inform)

Just for You

Reflect on the types of writing that you do, and then try something different. For example, if most of your writing is serious and intended to inform readers, try writing a humorous story or letter meant to entertain your reader.

Name _____ Date _____

Writers write with a purpose.

You can always do a better job if you know what you're doing and why you're doing it. This holds true with writing, too. Before writers begin putting words on paper, they ask themselves, "What do I want my readers to learn or to do as a result of reading my words?" Writers stay focused on the *why* of writing because they always write with a purpose.

Read for a Purpose, Too

Make a list of several things you have read recently. Try to include a variety of writing, such as:

- a chapter book
- a magazine article
- your social studies textbook
- a letter to the editor
- the newspaper comics
- a recipe
- an advertisement
- your teacher's comments on your homework
- a list of family chores

Now think about why you read each piece and what the writer's purpose was. Specifically, what did the writer want you to learn or do after reading? Try to identify examples of all five categories of writing: to request, inform, teach, persuade, and entertain.

Have It Five Ways!

- **Choose a topic that you are familiar with, for example, your pet, computer games, swimming, and so on.**
- **Now think about the five purposes of writing: to request, inform, teach, persuade, and entertain.**
- **Write five separate paragraphs about your topic, one written for each purpose. Before you begin to write, plan and organize your ideas using lists or webs. For example, jot down aspects of your topic that might be entertaining or humorous.**

Writers are readers.

Writers are avid readers, and they read voraciously! Writers learn and gain inspiration from reading a wide variety of styles and genres of books, as well as newspapers, magazines, signs, advertisements—in fact, just about anything in print!

Literature Connection

- *Author Talk* edited by Leonard S. Marcus and Judy Blume
- *How Writers Work: Finding a Process That Works for You* by Ralph Fletcher

Teacher Tip

On the following Student Activity Page students are asked to record unusual words in their writer's notebooks and to think about which stories, poems, and other types of writing inspire them and why. Discuss the important connection between avid reading and writing.

Making the Connection

- Invite students to look at the illustration on the card and discuss its message. Students should notice that since the boy is holding a pencil, he is probably writing, but he has stopped to consult the dictionary. They should also notice the other types of writing pictured in the bubbles—newspapers, books, magazines, and a Braille reader.

- Explain that writers love to read. They read all sorts of things. They often read to find information for their own writing, as the boy in the illustration is doing. But writers also read for enjoyment, inspiration, and new ideas. They read to discover different writing styles, unusual text formats, new vocabulary, and creative use of imagery.

- Tell students that writers read everything—from novels, to essays, to newspapers, to billboards, to cereal boxes! Ask students to name different kinds of reading they have done. List them on chart paper.

Connecting to Real Life

- Share author Gary Paulsen's advice for kids who want to write: "Read. . . Read like a wolf eats!. . . and carry a book with you all the time" (*Author Talk,* Section 12). Discuss the meaning of this powerful simile with students. Be sure to include the ideas of quantity and variety in the discussion.

- Bring in a wide variety of print materials that you have read in recent weeks. Include books, magazines, newspapers, crossword puzzles, poems, recipes, newsletters, posters, and food labels. Explain why you read each one and share interesting details that you learned. Then point out ways that your reading might inspire your own writing.

Just for You

Give yourself the gift of time to read! Somewhere in your busy schedule, carve out time each day to read for pleasure. Choose a variety of authors, genres, and styles, and keep a log of what you've read and titles you plan to read. Occasionally, share an excerpt or summary of your reading with students, letting them experience writing that excites, moves, or inspires you.

Writers are readers.

Author Karen Cushman tells writers "to read a lot and write a lot . . . it's like exercising muscles" (*Author Talk*, Section 3). Exercise *your* reading muscles by reading widely and often, both for enjoyment and to become a better writer.

Wonderful Words

Writers must be "in love with" language, Jane Yolen says. "Words are so powerful. They're tools we use for digging and, at the same time, they're the treasure waiting to be found," says James Howe (*Author Talk*, Section 6).

In your writer's notebook, start a list of great words you come across while reading. Look for words that are unusual or striking— words that speak to *you*. Who knows when you'll have a need to use "shimmering," "harrowing," or "persnickety" in your writing?

Surrounded by Words

Ralph Fletcher says, "I like to have certain books within easy reach when I write. I use books (novels and poetry) for inspiration. Other books (dictionary, thesaurus, and a book on grammar and usage) are important resources, too. When I'm putting words to paper I like to know that there are plenty of other words close by" (*How Writers Work: Finding a Process That Works for You,* Chapter 1).

1. **What stories, poems, and other types of writing inspire you? Which books made a deep impression on you? Make a section in your writer's notebook to keep track of what you read that is special to you.**
2. **Then write brief notes about *how* or *why* each piece inspired you (language? ideas? style? subject?).**
3. **If possible, create a place to write where you are surrounded by writing that inspires you.**

Writers persuade.

Persuasive writers can influence the way people think and act. In order to develop and use this powerful talent, writers need to know how to support their opinions with convincing facts.

Making the Connection

- Ask students to study the picture on the card. What do they imagine the boy is thinking about? (which person to vote for) Have students discuss how he can decide (listen to what both candidates have to say and see who is the most persuasive). Ask students to predict the kinds of information the candidates may use to persuade voters.

- Review the difference between fact and opinion. Then point out that persuasive writers express their personal opinions and try to convince readers to share those opinions. Ask students to express opinions about a school-related topic, such as whether it is better to bring or buy lunch. Ask students from each side of the issue to state facts and examples to support their opinions.

Connecting to Real Life

- Point out that advertising writers are skilled persuasive writers. Have students work in small groups to look at advertisements in magazines. Ask them to identify different strategies the ad writers use to persuade, such as using celebrities to promote products, persuasive language, facts, and statistics.

- Have students share times when they were verbally persuasive. For example, they may have convinced their parents to change a rule or persuaded a teacher to eliminate a homework assignment. Have them identify and share the techniques they used. Explain that the same techniques can be used in persuasive writing.

Just for You

Sometimes, the most challenging person to persuade is you. Think of something beneficial or enjoyable that you have considered doing, but have not yet accomplished. For example, the time commitment involved may have kept you from taking a photography class. Write a persuasive letter to convince yourself to take action.

Writers persuade.

Writing can be a powerful tool for convincing people to share an opinion or act in a certain way. However, writing only has that power if it is supported by facts and examples. Use these activities to build your persuasive writing skills.

Make Suggestions

Writers use many techniques to persuade their readers. They may mention famous people who agree with them. They may use statistics or persuasive language. To write strong persuasive pieces, you need to know the tricks of the trade.

Read several newspaper editorials and find an issue that interests you. Identify persuasive techniques the writer used. List other kinds of information he or she could use to make the argument stronger.

Remember Your Audience

Do you ever wish you could change your parents' or friends' minds? Try writing some persuasive paragraphs to get some results.

1. **Think of some things that you want to persuade someone to do. Maybe you want to convince your parents to let you stay up later on Friday nights, or maybe you want to persuade a friend to help you rake up the leaves in your backyard.**
2. **Choose two ideas. One idea should be aimed at one audience, such as a parent or a teacher. The other idea should be aimed at another audience, such as a friend, a sister, or a brother.**
3. **For each idea, make a chart to organize your thoughts. Use these headings:**
   - **my opinion or idea**
   - **facts to back up my opinion**
   - **arguments my reader might have**
   - **answers to those arguments**
4. **Write a persuasive paragraph for each of your ideas. Be sure each paragraph has an introduction, a body, and a conclusion.**
5. **Share your paragraphs with the person or people you want to persuade.**

Writers aren't always inspired.

Every writer has experienced writer's block and has times when inspiration is lacking. When this happens, writers don't give up. Instead, they turn to a variety of strategies to find fresh writing ideas and get their creative juices flowing.

Making the Connection

- Ask students to look at the illustration on the card and discuss how it relates to the strategy. Discuss with students the emotions reflected on the girl's face. Ask them why she became so frustrated. Suggest that this writer, like all writers, has frustrating times when words come with difficulty and inspiration is lacking.

- Have students describe strategies they might use to get past difficult times in their writing and rediscover inspiration. They might suggest brainstorming, webbing, informal outlining, making lists, clustering, and free writing. List ideas on chart paper.

Connecting to Real Life

- Explain that even very successful professional writers experience writer's block, but they don't let that stop them. Madeline L'Engle says, "I think you must write constantly, whether you feel like it or not" (*Pauses: Autobiographical Reflections of 101 Creators of Children's Books* by Lee Bennett Hopkins, Section 29).

- Remind students that most writers keep a writer's notebook, and they turn to it for ideas and inspiration when looking for writing topics, memories, or even just a colorful word or phrase. Have students share ways they have found inspiration for writing from their notebooks.

Just for You

You, too, will have days when writing is difficult. It helps to remember that writer's block is an experience shared by *all* writers. When it hits you, try this: Go for a walk to sharpen your observation skills, and listen to snatches of conversation around you for ideas. At times like this, it's more important than ever to continue to add tidbits, however small, to your writer's notebook.

Writers aren't always inspired.

You sit down. You're ready to write. Oh no! Your mind is blank—just like the piece of paper in front of you. What do you do?

Try a Brainstorming Exercise

When you just can't think of a topic, try this brainstorming exercise.

Start with one word. Below it, list a word related to the first word. One by one, list words as they come to mind. For example, "friend" may lead to "Joey"—then "hockey"—"broken stick"— "money"—"pet-sitting," and so on. This technique may yield ideas for your writing.

Pick a Prewriting Strategy

Choose one or more of these tried-and-true prewriting strategies to get your ideas flowing and your pencil moving.

List Brainstorm and list topic ideas—even ones that seem far-fetched. You never know what an idea will lead to until you let yourself think about it.

Web Start with one idea or word. Write it down and circle it. Add related words or ideas branching out around it.

Writer's Notebook or Topics List If you already have these tools, don't forget to use them!

Conference Explore ideas with a partner.

Read Collect a few of your favorite books or magazines to review. An idea may jump out at you!

Writers investigate and collect facts.

Writers are interested in a wide range of topics. Because they are naturally curious about the world around them, writers enjoy investigating and collecting facts about new topics. They use a variety of information sources to find answers to the questions they have.

Literature Connection

a selection of nonfiction books by Seymour Simon

Teacher Tip

- Writers find interesting facts to include in their writing. The following Student Activity Page instructs students to research a topic and use the information they find in a short story, letter, or poem. Encourage students to share their writing with the class.
- It is important to remember that gathering information on a topic does not always need to result in a finished story or report. The search for information is a writing activity in itself. Instead of reports, you might ask students to submit learning logs, interview questions on a subject, research notes, informal outlines, or just share the information with you or the class.

Making the Connection

- Have students look at the card, and ask, "How does the illustration represent writers investigating and collecting facts?" Students' responses should include the observation that the girl is rappelling down a "mountain of information." Ask students if they can think of sources of information writers might find useful. List their responses on chart paper. Sources may include books, magazines, computers, school, newspapers, radio, television, conversations, and so on.

- As a group activity, make a list of topics about which students would like to learn more. Ask students what they would like to know about these topics. Discuss different ways to gather information on some of the topics. Students' responses should include nonfiction books, encyclopedias, newspapers, magazines, the Internet, people, and so on.

Connecting to Real Life

- Bring a selection of Seymour Simon's nonfiction books into the classroom. Review the wide variety of topics he writes about—habitats, animals, planets, machines, and so on. Ask students how Mr. Simon knows so much about so many different topics. Point out that most writers do extensive research on each topic they write about and, through their research, become much more knowledgeable about that topic.

- Emphasize that a good piece of fictional writing needs to be as accurate in its details as nonfiction is. Explain to students that if they want to write a story about an animal, they will need to know many facts about the animal, such as what it eats, where it lives, when it sleeps, and how it hunts for food.

Just for You

List three sources of information you consult daily. Write down one interesting item from each source. Develop one of the ideas into a short informational piece.

Name _____ Date _____

Writers investigate and collect facts.

Author Seymour Simon never met a science subject he didn't like. In fact, he has written more than 200 books, including books on the human body, animals, weather, and volcanoes. How does Seymour Simon know so much about so many different topics? Like all writers, Mr. Simon must do research to learn about a new topic. Here is a research activity for you.

Become an Expert

What are some topics you would like to learn more about? Maybe you'd like to learn about volcanoes or a favorite author.

1. **In your journal or writer's notebook, make a list of "Topics I Would Like to Learn More About."**

2. **Then choose one of the topics to investigate. In your writer's notebook, list all the facts you already know about that topic.**

3. **On another page, list some of the questions you have or things you would like to know about the topic.**

4. **Select one or two of your key questions and try to find the answers. Then get busy investigating all you can about that topic.**

5. **Take notes about the facts you learn. Make sure to keep a list of each source of information you use and what you learned from each one.**

6. **Now that you've done some research about your topic, you are ready to write. Read through your notes. Of the facts you have collected, which are the most interesting?**

7. **Consider how you would like to present this information to your readers. How can you get them interested in the topic, too? Use your information in a short story, a letter to a friend, or in a poem.**

8. **Finally, check over your work, making sure you have used information correctly and chosen the right words to create a picture in your reader's mind.**

Writers are storytellers.

A realistic fiction writer may tell a story of a child moving to a new neighborhood. A fantasy writer may spin a tale of talking rabbits. A history writer may recount the life of a talented inventor. Whatever the story, a good storyteller develops a plot that keeps readers turning the pages. Use these activities to build your students' storytelling skills.

Making the Connection

- Tell students to study the picture on the card. Discuss the image (a girl imagining herself winning a ski race). Ask students to imagine the story the girl might tell. Have them suggest ideas of what the story might be about.

- Review the elements of any good story—characters, setting, and a plot with a conflict or problem to be solved. For each of these story elements, have students brainstorm details the girl pictured on the card might include, such as descriptions of other racers, the temperature outside, the feel of the snow under the skis, and a problem the girl must overcome to win the race.

Connecting to Real Life

- Share with students Ralph Fletcher's words about writing stories: "An essential element of narrative is that something happens. Something changes. Something goes wrong." Ask students to discuss what this statement tells them about being storytellers. Then have them suggest everyday events or experiences, such as eating breakfast. Point out that the secret to turning an ordinary event into an interesting story is having characters encounter a problem or an unexpected turn of events that creates suspense or tension. Have them brainstorm how things could change or go wrong in one of the activities they identified.

- Explain that both fiction and nonfiction can have elements of good storytelling. Share that Jean Fritz writes about real people, including Patrick Henry and Thomas Jefferson. She tells the stories of the dramatic and adventurous things that happened to these individuals. Suggest to students that they might consider using a historical figure as a character for a story.

Just for You

Your life as a teacher is rich with story ideas. In your writer's notebook, make a habit of recording funny, touching, and dramatic incidents involving students and adults you encounter daily.

Name _____ Date _____

Writers are storytellers.

Have you ever kept on reading a book past your bedtime because you just *had* to find out what happened next? How do authors get you to care so much about characters and situations? The secret is in building an interesting plot. These activities help you tell stories that keep your readers turning the pages.

Got a Problem?

Good plots involve a problem or conflict that must be resolved. The conflict can be internal, such as a decision to be made between characters, as in friends who disagree; or between a character and nature, such as a person stranded on a desert island.

Title a section of your writer's notebook "Story Situations." When unexpected happenings, problems, or changes in plans occur in your own life, record these in your notebook as potential story problems or conflicts. Later, make notes about possible solutions or resolutions to these problems or conflicts. Refer to your notebook the next time you are looking for plot ideas.

Get Organized

There are many ways to organize a good story. Try this sequence to turn one of the situations you identified in the previous activity into an exciting and interesting story.

1. **Set the scene.**
2. **Introduce the main characters.**
3. **Identify a problem or conflict the characters encounter.**
4. **Describe two or three attempts to solve the problem or conflict.**
5. **Tell how the problem or conflict is successfully resolved.**
6. **Explain how the characters changed or what they learned.**

Writers learn from other writers.

Many professional authors say that reading is the most important thing young authors can do to become better writers. Experienced and beginning writers alike learn about techniques, words, and styles by reading the works of professional writers—and the writing of their own peers. These activities encourage students to learn from other writers.

Literature Connection

- *The Other Side* by Jacqueline Woodson
- *Dealing with Dragons* by Patricia Wrede

Teacher Tip

Writers can make their own work better by reading the work of other writers. The following Student Activity Page encourages students to read the work of an author they enjoy and to share ideas with fellow writers in their class. They will then incorporate the new ideas and techniques into their own writing.

Making the Connection

- Ask students to discuss why the writer on the card is surrounded by books as he writes. Ask, "How can reading the works of different authors help us become better writers? What can we learn from other writers?"

- Remind students that just as beginning artists learn a lot about art from studying the work of famous artists, young writers can learn a lot about writing from studying the work of other authors. Also, discuss *plagiarism* with students. Remind them that while it is acceptable to imitate the style and techniques of other writers, it is never acceptable to copy their work word for word.

Connecting to Real Life

- Jacqueline Woodson, author of *The Other Side,* says, "I think that other authors taught me how to write." She says she read books she liked and decided, "I want to write like this one day." As students read independently, have them note in their writer's notebooks the names of writers they admire and how those writers might affect their own writing process.

- Writers learn by talking with other writers. Patricia Wrede, author of *Dealing with Dragons,* used to meet with six other writers who were trying to get their first writing published. This group, called the Scribblies, learned about writing from each other. Ask students what they have learned about writing from classmates.

Just for You

Use index cards as bookmarks for your leisure reading books. As you read, jot down interesting words, phrases, and techniques the author used. File the cards so you can refer to them when you need inspiration.

Name _____ Date _____

Writers learn from other writers.

Think of your favorite author. What would you like to ask that person about writing? You may not have a chance to actually talk with your favorite authors, but you can learn a lot from them by reading what they write. You can also learn a lot about writing from your peers.

Read Other Writers

Samuel Johnson, the great eighteenth-century writer, once said, "The greatest part of a writer's time is spent reading." As a writer, you need to read, read, and read! Follow these steps to learn from other authors:

1. **Choose an author whose books you enjoy. Read all or part of several of his or her books.**
2. **Make a list of things that are similar in all of the author's books you read.**
3. **Use at least one of the styles, ideas, or techniques you learned from your selected author to write a short essay, poem, or story.**

Learn from Your Classmates

You can learn from professional writers—but sometimes you can learn more from the writers in your own classroom.

1. **Exchange samples of writing with a classmate.**
2. **Take notes in your writer's notebook on interesting words or techniques your classmate used that you might like to try in future writing.**
3. **Try using some ideas from your notes in a draft you are currently working on.**
4. **After you have tried a particular technique, meet with the classmate who inspired you to try it. Decide together how well it worked in your writing.**
5. **Together discuss other techniques one or both of you might try.**

Writers write about people.

Literature Connection

- *Author Talk* edited by Leonard S. Marcus and Judy Blume
- *26 Fairmount Avenue* by Tomie dePaola
- *The Moon and I* by Betsy Byars

Teacher Tip

On the following Student Activity Page students are asked to write about a fictional character based on a person they know. They are also asked to write from another character's point of view and to write about someone they admire. Before students begin writing, discuss the importance of characters and how a writer can find inspiration through observing people.

Writers are people-watchers, and they get inspiration for writing by observing all the different people around them. Writers know that family, friends, neighbors, teammates, and even casual acquaintances can become characters in their fictional writing, or possibly the subject of a nonfiction piece.

Making the Connection

- Ask students to look at the card and describe the people in the picture. Discuss what each person's appearance and behavior might suggest about him or her. Then ask, "Do any of these people remind you of someone you know? In what ways?" Students' responses should include some inferences about the characters based on appearance and actions.

- Explain to students that writers write best when they write about what they know.

- Explain that a real person can be the inspiration for a fictional character or the subject of a nonfiction piece, such as a biography or a true story about something the person experienced.

- Point out that almost everyone is interested in knowing, hearing, and reading about other people. Have students share ideas about people they know who would make good writing subjects for fiction or nonfiction.

Connecting to Real Life

- Share and discuss the following quotation by Laurence Yep with students: "Working in our family store, and getting to know our customers, I learned early on how to observe and listen to people, how to relate to others. It was good training for a writer" (*Author Talk,* Section 15).

- Share parts of Tomie dePaola's Newbery Medal–winning autobiography, *26 Fairmount Avenue.* Point out the real people from dePaola's autobiography who also appear in his picture books (*Nana Upstairs & Nana Downstairs* and *Tom*).

Just for You

In *A Year in Provence,* Peter Mayle writes amusing, detailed descriptions of the many local people that he meets and befriends. Note how he builds each episode of the book around the charmingly eccentric people that he writes about. Try writing a story or vignette based on an encounter with someone you know.

Writers write about people.

You couldn't get along without other people—and most people wouldn't want to! Think about the people you know. Each person is unique and has special qualities that provide great inspiration for writers.

People Are Number 1!

In her autobiography, *The Moon and I*, Betsy Byars includes many stories about people she has known, including some memorable characters from her childhood. Byars says, "... even though the plot comes first, it is not the most important thing. The characters are the key to the story. They unlock the plot. They make it happen. So the characters, for me, are the most important element" (*The Moon and I*, Chapter 7).

1. **Write a paragraph describing a person you know.**
2. **Then think about how you might use this person as a story character.**
3. **Write a description of the fictional character based on the real person you know. Feel free to adapt or exaggerate the person's character traits, behavior, and appearance.**

Turn It Around

People tell stories every day, and most good stories involve people. Try telling a story from another person's perspective!

1. **Think of something that happened to a friend or relative.**
2. **Try to put yourself in this person's place—imagine the story is happening to you.**
3. **Write the story as if you were this person, from his or her point of view.**

Worth Writing About

Choose a real person you admire. Brainstorm words and phrases that describe the person, and organize them in a web. Then, using ideas from your web, write a personal profile. As part of this nonfiction piece, include an explanation of why you admire the person.

Writers wonder.

Writers are people who let their minds wander and wonder. By letting their imaginations run freely and asking *what if* questions, writers turn their "wonderings" into words. These activities help students foster and craft the art of "wondering."

Literature Connection

- *Meet the Authors and Illustrators, Vol. II* by Deborah Kovacs and James Preller
- *TV Sal and the Game Show from Outer Space* by Sheldon Oberman

Teacher Tip

Writers use their sense of wonder to find inspiration for their writing. The following Student Activity Page instructs students to write a paragraph based on their wonderings about the future. You might want to brainstorm with the class to create a list of things they might be curious about.

Making the Connection

- Invite students to look at the card and discuss its message (Sarah has an important characteristic of good writers—she wonders). Have students explain why it is important for writers to wonder. What does wondering bring to a writer's work? Ask students to list things that make them wonder.

- Explain that many questions people wonder about do not have answers that can be found by doing research. Have students review their lists to see which questions can be researched and answered, and which cannot. Encourage students to use their imaginations and writing skills to make up funny, scary, or interesting answers to the questions they could not find answers to. Ask volunteers to share their answers.

Connecting to Real Life

- Daniel Pinkwater, author of many children's books, says that the words *what if* are the greatest and only trick to writing fiction. He gives the example of a child shopping for a turkey for Thanksgiving, "What if he ends up buying a 266-pound chicken?" (*Meet the Authors and Illustrators,* Vol. II by Deborah Kovacs and James Preller) Ask students to discuss stories that could be written around this idea.

- Tell students that Sheldon Oberman also believes in the power of *what if.* His Web site (http://www.sheldonoberman.com/faq) encourages young writers to ask *what if* after reading a book. For instance, Oberman's *TV Sal and the Game Show from Outer Space* ends with the main character returning from outer space. Oberman asks, "What if Sal took his family back to outer space with him?" He suggests writing a sequel to answer the question. Ask students to list *what if* questions about books they have read.

Just for You

What makes you wonder? Write a short essay in which you explore the answer to one of your own *what if* questions.

Name _____ Date _____

Writers wonder.

What if you could travel through time? What if you could understand your cat's language? Use your sense of wonder—and your imagination—to get ideas for your writing.

Wonder Why

Asking yourself *why* and *what if* is a great way to spark story ideas.

1. Flip through a nonfiction book. Pay attention to the pictures and headings.
2. Notice the *why* and *what if* questions that pop into your mind. For example, if you were looking at information about wind in a science book and saw a picture of a weather vane, you might ask yourself, "Why are weather vanes often shaped like roosters?"
3. Write as many questions as you can. Then choose one and brainstorm answers. Draft a story or poem using the idea.

Journey Through Time

You may wonder about the future. There is no way to know for sure the answers to what you wonder, but you can use your imagination and wonder about what it will be like.

1. Think of something about the future that makes you curious. For example, maybe you wonder what cars will look like in fifty years or if we will be vacationing on Mars or Jupiter.
2. Then let your mind wander and explore different possibilities.
3. Write a paragraph that answers your "wonderings" about the future and share the wonderings with a friend.
4. Hang your finished writing on a bulletin board titled "Our Future . . . Maybe."

Writers write about special moments.

Everyone's life has special moments. Writing about important events that have personal significance is more than a way to preserve a memory; such writing gives readers a picture that is real, honest, and rich with details.

Literature Connection

- *Owl Moon* by Jane Yolen
- *The Random House Book of Poetry for Children* selected by Jack Prelutsky

Teacher Tip

On the following Student Activity Page students are asked to write about a special moment. Before students begin writing, discuss the fact that writing about a special moment is a way to preserve the memory. Stress the importance of including details to reflect the feelings associated with the moment.

Making the Connection

- Invite students to look at the card and discuss what is happening in the picture. (A large crowd cheers as a soccer goalie reaches up and blocks a goal.) Ask students to speculate about how the goalie is feeling, and if they can remember a time when they felt this way. Point out that this is a special moment for the goalie and this feeling could provide inspiration for a poem, story, or nonfiction article.

- Explain that everyone has special moments—ordinary lives are full of them! If an event evokes strong feelings—excitement, pride, even sorrow or regret—then it is a good subject to write about. Have students identify and discuss some special moments in their lives. What feelings are associated with each of these special moments?

Connecting to Real Life

- If possible, bring in a journal entry or reflection that you have written about a significant moment in your life. Read it to the students and ask them to think about the details you have included. What feelings are evoked by the writing?

- Share examples of writing about special moments that have a strong sense of setting and/or mood. For example, read Jane Yolen's picture book *Owl Moon* and Judith Viorst's poem "Since Hanna Moved Away" (*The Random House Book of Poetry for Children* selected by Jack Prelutsky).

- Have student pairs share their own stories of special moments with each other.

Just for You

A special moment worth writing about is special precisely because of the writer's feelings. In choosing a special moment to write about, consider how you feel. It is your feelings, and not the drama of the moment, that will make the writing powerful.

Writers write about special moments.

Writers know that special moments and memories from their own lives provide excellent ideas for writing. What memories do you cherish? What events have made you feel proud, happy, or sad? No one else's special moments and memories are the same as yours.

Remember Your Own Special Moments

Think about special moments in your life. Most of them will probably be happy, but some may be sad, funny, or scary. Remember, even if you think your life is "ordinary," you will always experience moments that are special to you. Using your own life experiences will help you write with feeling.

In your writer's notebook, list four or five special moments. Next to each, jot down where the event happened. Then make notes about how you felt during the event. What made it special to you?

A Small Moment in Time

Choose one special moment from your list. Spend a few minutes remembering the event. Think about the details of what happened—the setting, the general mood, and how you felt.

1. **Make a time line of the event. Include as many details as possible.**
2. **Using your time line, try to focus on the most important part of the event. Eliminate the parts of the time line before and after this part.**
3. **Write a story, nonfiction article, or poem about this small, special moment in time. Include specific details, and tell why this moment was so special.**

Writers notice little things.

Teacher Tip

On the following Student Activity Page students are asked to notice and list details in their environment to develop their "writer's eyes" and then to write a paragraph rich in sensory details. Discuss with students how the awareness of the details in their day-to-day lives will help them become descriptive writers.

Writers pay attention to the world around them and are aware of all the little things in their day-to-day lives. Writers notice and use sights, smells, sounds, textures, and tastes in their writing to make it rich in detail and powerful.

Making the Connection

- Ask students to look carefully at the illustration on the card. Then turn the card over, and ask them to try to remember as many details from the picture as possible. As a group, list all the things students remember about the picture.

- Explain that writers are aware of the world around them. They notice little things like the many details in the picture. They pay attention to what they see and make mental notes. Later, writers recall these little things and use them in various ways to spark a story idea, to create a realistic background, and to develop interesting characters.

Connecting to Real Life

- Share little things that you have observed and noted in your journal or writer's notebook. If possible, discuss how you plan to use one of these details in your writing. Encourage students to share specific things they have observed with their "writer's eyes."

- Point out how Cynthia Rylant uses a "little thing" (a character's use of one word) to paint a striking picture of a character in *Missing May*: "May was gardening when she died. That's the word she always used: *gardening.* Everybody else in Fayette County would say they were going out to work in the garden, and that's the picture you'd get in your mind—people out there laboring and sweating and grunting in the dirt. But Aunt May *gardened,* and when she said it your mind would see some lovely person in a yellow-flowered hat snipping soft pink roses, with little robins landing on her shoulders" (*Missing May,* Chapter 2).

Just for You

Find time to sit in a familiar place and really *notice* your surroundings. Use all your senses to really appreciate this special place.

Writers notice little things.

Stop, look, and listen! Writers are sharp observers and listeners. They notice countless details and other "little things" that can be used to bring life to their writing.

Train Your "Writer's Eyes"

Ralph Fletcher explains that "Effective writing starts with 'honest, specific, accurate' information." Details from your own experiences and observations can make your writing honest, specific, and accurate.

1. **Set aside half an hour to help develop your "writer's eyes." During this time, use your senses. Be aware of sounds, smells, and sights. Try to notice, carefully observe, and record several unusual "little things" in the familiar world of your school environment—your classroom, school yard, auditorium, cafeteria, and so on.**
2. **Make a list in your writer's notebook of the details you noticed.**
3. **Exchange lists with one another to see what details your classmates noticed.**

Little Things, Big Meaning

Specific writing is powerful writing. The "little things" have great impact.

1. **Think of an experience that was especially meaningful or important to you. Try to remember as many details as you can about the experience. What did you see, feel, smell, taste, and hear?**
2. **Write a paragraph about the experience, including specific sensory details. Make your writing powerful by including the "little things" that you noticed.**

Writers write about the unexpected and unusual.

Writers use the unexpected and unusual events in their lives as inspiration for writing. Many of these events can be positive, such as your basketball team winning a game or earning a reward for finding a lost pet. Other events, such as an illness or the death of a pet, are negative.

Literature Connection

- *Hurricane* by David Weisner
- *Habibi* by Naomi Shihab Nye
- *How My Parents Learned to Eat* by Ina R. Friedman

Teacher Tip

On the following Student Activity Page students are asked to write about an unusual or unexpected personal experience. Discuss with students how any unusual or unexpected event, both positive and negative, can be an inspiration for writing. Explain that writing about such events will evoke strong feelings and provide compelling reading.

Making the Connection

- Have students look at the card and ask them how the picture represents the unexpected and unusual. Responses should reflect the understanding that the boy, who looks happy and proud, won a prize at a fair for growing an unusually large pumpkin. Point out that this unusual event would make a good writing topic for him.

- Explain that many stories are based on authors' unexpected and unusual experiences. Discuss with students that such stories make good writing topics because these events evoke strong feelings, provide drama, and so on. Ask students to identify stories or poems they have read that are about unexpected or unusual events, both positive and negative.

Connecting to Real Life

- Bring in examples of writing about unusual or unexpected events, such as *Hurricane* by David Weisner and *Habibi* by Naomi Shihab Nye. Ask students to suggest unusual or unexpected experiences they might write about. What was the setting? What impact did it have on the event? What feelings did the event produce?

- Explain that unusual problems or events, and the ways that a person chooses to deal with them, make good stories. As an example, you might share Ina R. Friedman's picture book *How My Parents Learned to Eat*. Tell students that the author wrote this book after she and a Japanese friend discussed their difficulties in "learning to eat." The unusual problem of learning the eating conventions of a different culture led to a very unusual and compelling story.

Just for You

Be open to unexpected events! Notice details, emotions, mood and how it changes, and participants' differing points of view as you deal with life's unexpected and unusual events. Jot down a few quick notes after the event while your memory is fresh. Later, experiment with writing about the event in different formats, such as poetry or nonfiction.

Writers write about the unexpected and unusual.

What unusual or unexpected things have happened to you recently? What surprising events, either good or bad, did you have to deal with? Put your experiences to good use, as professional writers do, by including them in your writing.

What's Happened to <u>You</u> Lately?

Betsy Byars was working on a book when a black snake appeared on her front porch. She was so entranced by the snake, which she named Moon, that she accidentally deleted an entire chapter from her computer! But she later wrote another book, called *The Moon and I,* in which the snake plays an important part. What unusual, unexpected things could you write about?

1. **In your writer's notebook, list several ideas, including both positive things (making a team, winning a contest, finding a stray dog that you get to keep) and negative ones (getting lost, breaking an arm, having to change schools). Some events may have both negative and positive qualities.**
2. **Label the ideas as positive or negative. Since some events may have positive and negative qualities, label them "both."**

Use Your Experience

Choose one unusual or unexpected event from your list to write about. As you plan your writing, think about the following:

- **Where did the event take place? What is the importance of the setting? How did the setting affect the event?**
- **What were your feelings during the unexpected event? Be sure that your feelings (positive or negative) match the mood of your writing.**
- **Which writing format will best convey the mood you want to express—a poem, story, or nonfiction piece?**

Writers reread and rewrite.

Students need to understand that finished writing is writing that has gone through several revisions. An author needs to reread and rewrite his or her work, checking for clarity, language, details, and grammar. Encourage students to submit early drafts to find and correct problem areas. Rereading and rewriting are important steps on the way to a clear and polished final draft.

Literature Connection

How Writers Work: Finding a Process That Works for You by Ralph Fletcher

Teacher Tip

Writers often return to their work several times before achieving the finished product. The following Student Activity Page guides students through the process of revising and rewriting a draft. Have students break into groups to share their original and revised writing. Encourage students to discuss the changes made to the first draft.

Making the Connection

- Invite students to describe the illustrations on the card and discuss their significance. Be sure students understand that the writer is spending time working on the same piece of writing: rereading, rewriting, then coming back with a fresh perspective at a later time to repeat the process several more times.

- E. L. Konigsburg compared her writing process to the work of an oil painter. Oil paintings are reworked again and again, much like writing that is revisited and reworked several times. Together, discuss the advantages of a process that includes reworking or "touching up," followed by a time of rest or "letting it dry," followed by more reworking.

Connecting to Real Life

- Copy a first draft of your own writing onto an overhead transparency. With a different colored pen, add your first round of revisions and corrections. Display the transparency and discuss the revisions that you made and the reasons for each change, addition, or deletion. Then share your thinking aloud as you make a second round of revisions, using another pen color. Explain that you will put the writing away for a while and then repeat the process of rereading and rewriting, perhaps choosing a focus such as adding details or correcting grammar.

- Share Drew Lamm's upbeat attitude toward revising: "I'm wild for revising. Love it. It's like playing! . . . Once you discover that you have something, you can stop sweating and start messing around with it—revise" (quoted in *How Writers Work* by Ralph Fletcher, Chapter 7).

Just for You

Look in your writer's notebook and find a piece you haven't read in a while. Reread it—and rewrite it. Repeat the process until you are satisfied with the piece.

Writers reread and rewrite.

Who knows your story best? You do, of course! That's why your own judgment is so valuable during the process of revising your writing. Once your first draft is written, use the reread-and-rewrite strategy to be sure your writing says what you want it to say, in the best way possible.

Step One: Meaning Comes First

Choose a recent draft of your writing. As you reread your draft, ask yourself these questions:

- **Does this make sense?**
- **Is there anything that doesn't belong?**
- **Is important information missing?**

During this stage of the rewriting process, feel free to cross things out, add phrases, change words, and move sections. Use a colored pencil to make changes. Then set your work aside so you can tackle Step Two with fresh eyes.

Step Two: Fine-Tuning

Now that you know your writing makes sense and says what you want it to say, shift your focus to how you've written your story or message. Reread your draft. Then consider these questions:

- **Who is my audience? Have I met their needs?**
- **Does my writing "show" rather than "tell"?**
- **Have I included details and "little things" that will make my writing believable and realistic?**
- **Have I thought about my words and chosen words that are precise and powerful?**
- **Does my voice come through in the writing?**

Use a different colored pencil than you did in Step One to make additional revisions. Then rewrite your draft, and set it aside again.

Step Three: Final Clean Up

Now your writing makes sense and says what you want it to say in a way that pleases you. To make it perfect, reread it once more. This time, focus on spelling, grammar, and punctuation. Correct any mistakes, and rewrite one last time. Success!

Writers write about things that are important to them.

When writers choose topics they care about, their writing comes alive. By writing about things that inspire their hearts and minds, writers help readers see ordinary people, places, events, and things in new and interesting ways.

Literature Connection

- *The Hundred Penny Box* by Sharon Bell Mathis
- *The Remarkable Journey of Prince Jen* by Lloyd Alexander
- *My Side of the Mountain* and *The Cry of the Crow* by Jean Craighead George

Teacher Tip

Writers make their writing interesting by choosing topics that they care about. The following Student Activity Page guides students through the process of writing about a favorite object. Provide additional assistance to students who have difficulty brainstorming about their favorite object.

Making the Connection

- Show students the card and ask them what they think the pictures around the children represent (things that are important to them). Ask students to think about what these objects represent and why they might hold special meaning for the children. Have students identify and tell about any of the hobbies, skills, collections, or pets that are important to them, too.

- Show students three objects that are important to you—one from the past, one from the present, and one concerning a dream you have for the future. Share with students how you feel about the objects.

- Ask students to make time lines from their birth to their current age. Have them list, at appropriate points along the time lines, people, places, events, or things that have been important to them.

- Share the picture book *The Hundred Penny Box* by Sharon Bell Mathis. Read aloud the story of Aunt Dew and her box of memories. Show students a box in which you have placed intriguing items. Take out the objects, one by one. Ask students to imagine what special significance each one might hold for someone else.

Connecting to Real Life

- Tell students that the author Lloyd Alexander included a flute, a paint box, and a bronze bowl that he owned as a child in his story *The Remarkable Journey of Prince Jen*. Ask students to jot down three of their favorite objects. Encourage them to think about a way in which these articles might be woven into a story. Then have them share their ideas with a partner.

- Point out that author Jean Craighead George has featured many of her family pets in her stories. *My Side of the Mountain* was inspired by her experience of owning a falcon as a teenager, and *The Cry of the Crow* includes the antics of a crow that her son brought home.

Just for You

Think of a possession you would like to pass on to someone, now or in the future. Write a note to that person explaining why the object is important to you.

Writers write about things that are important to them.

This seems simple enough, but it may not be as easy as it sounds. You can probably name a favorite toy, a piece of clothing, or a keepsake without thinking very hard. But why is this object important to you? What words best describe your exact feelings about it? How can you help others understand your feelings?

Explore Your Feelings

Use a chart to explore why a certain object is important to you.

1. **First, write the name of a favorite object at the top of a blank page in your writer's notebook. Then list these headings down the left side: *Description, How I got it, My feelings, What it reminds me of, Facts I know about it, What it may mean to me in the future.***
2. **Finally, on the right side, make notes about each heading.**

Share Your Feelings

Write about the object and try to describe your feelings about it.

1. **First, try to learn more about your favorite thing. You can interview a family member or you can do research in a library or on the Internet. Find out about the object's history. Find out how other people feel about this type of item. Add what you learn to your chart.**
2. **Choose a way to share what you feel and what you've found out about your favorite thing. Use the ideas on your chart to write a poem, a story, or a song. Ask a friend or family member for ideas. Copy your writing onto a large index card.**
3. **Place the item, or a photograph or drawing of it, and the card on a display table in your classroom. Answer questions your classmates may have about your poem, story, or song, or about the object itself.**

Writers are all different.

Writers are unique, bringing different experiences and ways of thinking to their work. Since no two people are the same, good writers work hard at developing their own voices, writing about their own backgrounds, interests, and experiences, and making their writing direct, personal, and honest.

Making the Connection

- Ask students to look at the card. How does the illustration reflect the difference of writers? Students should note that, although there are similarities among all the people in the picture, it's easy to see that each student has unique interests. One plays violin, one skates, one paints and plays baseball, and so on.

- Explain that just as people have different interests, they also have individual and unique ways of thinking, speaking, and writing. In writing, an individual's "voice" is not only what he or she says but also *how* he or she says it. Writing with your own voice is honest and open; it lets the reader know who you are—in the same way an observer knows which student in the picture loves cheerleading and which one never leaves home without his skateboard.

Connecting to Real Life

- Read aloud excerpts from books with distinctive voices. You might choose *26 Fairmount Avenue* by Tomie dePaola, *A Long Way from Chicago: A Novel in Stories* by Richard Peck, or *Joey Pigza Loses Control* by Jack Gantos. Discuss how the authors use voice in each.

- Explore with students the differences in voice, and how each writer's unique writing is lively, believable, and powerful.

- Share the quotation, "Writing *with voice* is writing into which someone has breathed" (Peter Elbow, quoted by Fletcher in *What a Writer Needs,* Chapter 6). Together, discuss what this idea might mean.

Just for You

Voltaire said, "I don't agree with a word you say, but I will defend to the death your right to say it." While most would argue that this quotation is a reflection on freedom of speech, it could apply to voice also. Do you read books and stories with a lot of different voices? Do you try to write in different voices?

Literature Connection

- *26 Fairmount Avenue* by Tomie dePaola
- *A Long Way from Chicago: A Novel in Stories* by Richard Peck
- *Joey Pigza Loses Control* by Jack Gantos
- *What a Writer Needs* by Ralph Fletcher

Teacher Tip

On the following Student Activity Page students are asked to rewrite a journal entry for others to read and then to write about a meaningful topic in their own voice. Before students begin writing, discuss the concept of "voice" in writing as one's unique way of expressing thoughts and feelings. Stress the importance of writing with voice by contrasting different authors' styles.

Name _____ Date _____

Writers are all different.

There's no one else like you! You're a special individual with your own interests and experiences. Let your writing reflect the real you. Make your writing lively, honest, and powerful by writing in your own voice.

Let the World Hear Your Voice!

Ralph Fletcher says that one purpose of keeping a journal is to "provide a place to relax, to settle into a comfortable writing stride." He speaks about his "easy journal voice," which is relaxed because he is the sole audience. Then he tries to let some of his easy journal voice "leak into" the writing he does for publication (*What a Writer Needs*).

1. **Choose an entry in your writer's notebook that is written in your "easy journal voice."**
2. **Then rewrite the entry for others to read. You may edit and polish as necessary, but don't remove your voice! Remember to let your personal voice "leak into" your writing for readers to enjoy.**

If You Wouldn't Say It . . .

To help students understand voice, Mike Brusko says, "If you wouldn't say it that way, don't write it that way" (*Writing Rules!*). Write like you talk, and write about things you enjoy and know well.

1. **Choose a writing topic that is meaningful to you. Or choose a story idea that is based on a personal, memorable experience.**
2. **As you work, occasionally read your words aloud. Does the writing sound natural and lively? Is it in your own voice?**

Writers collect ideas.

Literature Connection

- *How Writers Work: Finding a Process That Works for You* by Ralph Fletcher
- *Quotations for Kids* edited by J. A. Senn
- *Scholastic Treasury of Quotations for Children* edited by Adrienne Betz
- *The Moon and I* by Betsy Byars

Teacher Tip

On the following Student Activity Page students are asked to begin collecting ideas to add to their writer's notebooks and then to write a paragraph based on a thought-provoking quotation of their choosing. Remind students that they can find inspiration for writing from a wide variety of sources, such as books, newspapers, television, magazines, movies, and so on. Encourage students to record ideas for writing on a regular basis.

Writers are eager to learn and think about new and different ideas. Writers know that ideas can come from newspapers, books, television, artwork, film, the Internet, and other people. Writers collect ideas in a writer's notebook, knowing that these ideas can be used in their writing in many different ways.

Making the Connection

- Invite students to look at the illustration on the card and discuss its meaning. Students' responses should indicate understanding that the boy with the pencil is a writer, and that he is noticing, thinking about, and remembering many different ideas. The sources of these ideas include a television news broadcast, a fiction book, a newspaper, and a conversation.

- Explain that writers are open to new ideas and opposing viewpoints, and they collect ideas from many different sources. Ask students to identify other sources of ideas and opinions in addition to those in the picture; for example, radio, films, fine art, magazines, advertisements, and the Internet.

Connecting to Real Life

- Tell students that when writers find an interesting idea, they record or "collect" it in a writer's notebook. Drew Lamm explains, "I'm a much more interesting person with my notebook than without it because it keeps me alert. . . . any idea that flies by gets a place to land" (quoted by Fletcher in *How Writers Work,* Chapter 7).

- Bring in a variety of newspaper and magazine clippings and photos that you have collected. Share ways that you have used (or might use) them in your writing.

- Discuss with students the reasons that a writer might want to collect different ideas, including opposing viewpoints or unpopular opinions. Help students understand the variety of ways a writer might make use of ideas collected in a writer's notebook. For example, an idea could become a writing topic, the opinion of a fictional character, or part of a persuasive argument.

Just for You

Do you always read the same newspaper or listen to the same news program? Try using alternate sources for a week. Seek out diverse news magazines. Be open to new ideas, and record your ideas and reactions in a journal or writer's notebook.

Writers collect ideas.

Do you enjoy collecting shells, baseball cards, or postcards? Writers have collections, too. Writers collect new, different, serious, and quirky ideas. Try these activities to get your own "idea collection" started.

Good Scraps!

Newbery Medalist Betsy Byars calls the ideas she collects for her writing "good scraps." She says, "Plenty of good scraps are as important in making a book as in the making of a quilt." Some scraps she has put into her books include a black snake on her front porch, a cat with a golden earring, and a gift-wrapped dime (*The Moon and I,* Chapter 7).

1. **In your writer's notebook, start your own list of "good scraps." Collect your ideas from as many different sources as possible, such as newspapers, movies, and overheard conversations.**
2. **Next to each idea in your list, jot down thoughts about how you might use it in your writing.**

What Do You Think?

The thoughts and ideas of many different people, past and present, can be found in books of quotations.

1. **Look through a book of quotations, such as *Quotations for Kids* (compiled and edited by J. A. Senn) or *Scholastic Treasury of Quotations for Children* (edited by Adrienne Betz).**
2. **Choose a quotation that strikes you as interesting, unusual, or thought provoking. It may express a sentiment that you agree or disagree with.**
3. **Write a paragraph about the idea, focusing on how *you* feel about it, and why.**

Writers don't always start at the beginning.

Sometimes writers just need to start writing to see where their ideas take them. By not worrying about finding the perfect beginning, a writer's ideas can ebb and flow and often bring out the writer's best work. A good technique for young writers to experiment with is to start a piece of writing in the middle or even at the end, and then go back to write the beginning later.

Literature Connection

Pauses: Autobiographical Reflections of 101 Creators of Children's Books by Lee Bennett Hopkins

Teacher Tip

Sometimes writers begin their writing in the middle of the piece, then go back to create an interesting beginning. The following Student Activity Page provides students with several techniques for crafting interesting story openings. Have students use one of these techniques to revise a paragraph of their own writing, and encourage volunteers to share the revised paragraph with the class.

Making the Connection

- Invite students to consider how the illustration on the card relates to the strategy. (The boy has a very large sandwich and is about to take a bite right in the middle.) Writing can seem large, too, and sometimes it makes sense to start right in the middle, in the juiciest, most appealing part.

- Ask students to think about and describe jobs or other activities they have started in the middle. Why did they choose this strategy? How did it work out?

- Together, explore reasons why it might sometimes be a good idea to start a piece of writing in the middle, or even at the end. For example, unsure how much to reveal, or in need of more information for a clear introduction, a writer may be stuck for a good beginning. Encourage students to plunge in and write about the main action or the ending. Then, as inspiration strikes, go back and write the beginning.

Connecting to Real Life

- Explain that writing a good beginning is challenging even for professional writers. Share Clyde Robert Bulla's experience with beginnings: "The opening paragraph is the hardest; sometimes I write as many as fifty or sixty before turning out one I can use" (*Pauses: Autobiographical Reflections of 101 Creators of Children's Books* by Lee Bennett Hopkins, Sections 20–26). Discuss reasons why beginnings can be so difficult for writers.

- Read aloud examples of beginnings that avoid the words *when* or *one*. Help students recognize and make a list of other options for beginnings, such as dialogue, sound effects, a character's thoughts, a quotation, a question, or an unusual fact.

Just for You

Try starting a poem or story from the middle or end. Then, go back and write the beginning. Did starting from a different point help you create a stronger opening?

Writers don't always start at the beginning.

Has this happened to you? You sit down, ready to write, and then find yourself unable to begin. Beginnings can be difficult, and writers have various ways of dealing with them. Sometimes it's wise just to plunge in at the middle or end and write the beginning later. It's also useful to keep alternatives for catchy beginnings in your writer's notebook.

Dive Right In!

When you start a piece of writing, don't let yourself get bogged down trying to find a perfect beginning. Instead, try skipping ahead to the part of the story that most excites or inspires you.

Dive in and start writing:
- **in the middle, where there is some surprise or dramatic action; or**
- **at the end, where you tie the pieces into a satisfying conclusion.**

Then, go back and write the beginning. Was it easier to start writing your story without worrying about crafting a good lead?

A New Beginning

Gather samples of your writing, and notice how each one begins. Are the beginnings similar? Do many begin with the common story-opening words *once, when,* or *one*?

On your next draft, experiment with a different kind of beginning. For ideas, look at the opening paragraphs of your favorite stories or choose an idea from the list below.

Technique	Example
sound effect	Cr–unch! I'd just stepped on the last cookie.
dialogue	"Dad! I passed the swimming test!"
question	How bad can a tornado be?
thought	Why did I agree to this, I wondered for the millionth time.
quotation	"Honesty is the best policy."

Writers describe.

Literature Connection

- *Ragweed: A Tale from Dimwood Forest* by Avi
- *California* by Ann Heinrichs
- *The Night Journey, Shadows in the Dawn: The Lemurs of Madagascar,* and *True North: A Novel of the Underground Railroad* by Kathryn Lasky

Teacher Tip

A writer's use of vivid descriptions can help a reader become more absorbed in the writer's work. The following Student Activity Page provides opportunities for students to enhance their descriptive writing skills. Students are guided to design the classroom of their dreams. They are also invited to write a character sketch for a real or imaginary person. Provide students with blank copies of the Character Traits Web on page 31 of the *Rigby Literacy Graphic Organizer Book.*

Have you ever shivered as you read about the icy expanses of Antarctica? Have you gasped when you read about a black cat pouncing out of the bushes? Writers bring their writing to life for their readers when they use vivid descriptions. Use these activities to help students bring anticipation, suspense, and imagery to their writing by using effective descriptions.

Making the Connection

- Have students study the card, and ask them what writers can learn from it. (Adding details gives readers a clearer picture.) Ask students to identify the elements that have been added to each description.

- Make sure students understand how word choice (exact nouns, vivid verbs, and specific, sensory adjectives and adverbs) can strengthen their descriptions. Have students create a word chart in their writer's notebooks where they record strong words they read or hear. Encourage them to refer to these word charts when they need help coming up with powerful and descriptive words.

Connecting to Real Life

- Explain that both fiction and nonfiction writers use descriptions. Read an example of descriptive fiction writing, such as the first few pages of Avi's *Ragweed: A Tale from Dimwood Forest.* Have students identify specific techniques the author uses to describe characters, setting, and action. Then read an example of descriptive nonfiction writing, such as the beginning of Chapter 3 in *California* by Ann Heinrichs. Have students explain how the author uses descriptive language to bring the topic of the book to life.

- Note that when author Kathryn Lasky *(The Night Journey, Shadows in the Dawn: The Lemurs of Madagascar,* and *True North: A Novel of the Underground Railroad)* was ten, she told her mother that she could not see the stars because of the "woolly" clouds in the "sheepback sky." Encourage students to use creative comparisons to describe some classroom objects.

Just for You

Close your eyes and create a mental image of a real or imaginary tranquil setting. Open your eyes and write a detailed description of what you visualized. Try to incorporate all five senses. Keep this description handy and read it whenever you need a quick "vacation."

Writers describe.

Would you rather watch a television show in black and white or in color?
Most people would say color because it is more exciting and true-to-life.
As a writer, your writing can seem like it is in black and white or in color.
It all depends on how much thought you put into describing people, places,
and things.

A Special Place

Design the classroom of your dreams in a short essay.

1. **Write a draft that answers questions such as:**
   - **What would you include if you could create a classroom that would make learning even more fun?**
   - **What kinds of equipment, materials, and decorations would be in the classroom?**
   - **How would teachers and students use the spaces, equipment, and furniture in the classroom?**
2. **After you have drafted your ideas, reread your description and ask yourself, "What adverbs and adjectives can I add to help my reader see, hear, feel, smell, and taste things in my classroom?" Revise your description to include sensory details.**

Create a Character Sketch

A character sketch is a description that tells how a person acts, thinks, and feels. Write a character sketch for a real or imaginary person.

1. **Prepare to write a description by making a Character Traits Web. Be sure to include physical traits as well as the character's actions and thoughts.**
2. **As you write your sketch, include exact nouns and vivid verbs to make the description come alive. For example, instead of writing, "His face moves when he laughs," write, "His sagging cheeks bounce and jiggle when he laughs."**
3. **Use your character sketch to inspire you to write a story or biography.**

Writers daydream and imagine.

Literature Connection

- *The Black Cauldron* by Lloyd Alexander
- *The Mystery of Mr. Nice: A Chet Gecko Mystery* by Bruce Hale
- *Sounder* by William Armstrong
- *In the Night Kitchen* by Maurice Sendak
- *Swimmy* by Leo Lionni

Teacher Tip

Writers use their imaginations to write about unreal things. The following Student Activity Page instructs students to write science fiction and fantasy stories, using organizers such as a sequence chain and a story elements chart. These can be found on pages 7 and 15, respectively, in the *Rigby Literacy Graphic Organizer Book*. You might want to model creating and completing these organizers for the class.

Todd Strasser, author of numerous young adult books, describes writing fiction as "sort of like being in a daydream all day long." Writers—particularly those who write fantasy and science fiction—use their imaginations to create whole new worlds. Encourage students to explore their imaginations to come up with their own dreamlike ideas for writing.

Making the Connection

- Ask students what the boy on the card is doing (creating a world in his mind). Have students discuss the setting he is imagining, who might live there, and what might happen. Explain that writers do not have to write about the real world; they can make up improbable, imaginary worlds.

- Mention that daydreaming can be an important part of writing. Play relaxing instrumental music. Have students close their eyes and daydream for a few minutes. Ask volunteers to share the ideas that floated through their heads that might be used to build stories.

Connecting to Real Life

- "Reading takes us where we want to go, to places we have never been," said Lloyd Alexander, who creates mythical worlds in books such as *The Black Cauldron*. Ask students to describe imaginary settings from books they have read. Suggest that they, too, can create imaginary places through their writing.

- Tell students that many authors, such as Bruce Hale, author of *The Mystery of Mr. Nice: A Chet Gecko Mystery*, use animals as characters in an attempt to make everyday life more interesting. Ask students to describe animals they know that might inspire ideas for characters in fantasy stories.

- Sometimes writers use their imaginations to fill in gaps. William Armstrong based *Sounder* on a family he knew as a boy. He did not know all the details of their lives, so he made up parts. Explain that students may combine real-life people, places, or events with imaginative ideas to weave stories together.

Just for You

Reread classic fantasy picture books, such as *In the Night Kitchen* by Maurice Sendak and *Swimmy* by Leo Lionni. Be sure to notice the fanciful illustrations. Use these images to inspire your own imaginative writing.

Name _____ Date _____

Writers daydream and imagine.

Do you like to daydream? What kinds of places do you see in your daydreams? What fantastic creatures do you envision? What magical powers do people have? As a writer, you can let your imagination give you the power to create fantastic new worlds.

Create a Science Fiction Story

Use the following steps to mix what you learn about science with your imagination to write a science fiction story.

1. **Think of facts you learned from science books, such as Mars is the fourth planet from the Sun.**
2. **Decide how you could mix true scientific information with made-up details to write a science fiction adventure. For example, you could learn facts about the planet Mars and then write about an imaginary Mars space station of the future.**
3. **Use a sequence chain to plan events that will take place in your story.**
4. **After you have finished a first draft, ask classmates if they have ideas about other true facts you could add to your story to make it more engaging.**

Write a Fantasy Story

Interesting stories include characters, settings, problems, and solutions. In a fantasy story, one or more of those parts is unreal.

1. **Draw a story elements chart. Decide which elements you will make unreal. For example, you might put your characters in a make-believe place or give them a problem that could not happen in real life.**
2. **Complete the chart to show the events that lead to the characters solving their problem.**
3. **Use the chart to write your story. Since your story will involve characters, settings, or problems that your readers have not experienced in real life, be sure to use vivid descriptions to explain how things look and what is happening.**

Writers get help.

Writers use many sources of help to improve their writing and to find answers to questions. They conference with peers, seek out suggestions from relatives, refer to reference materials and the Internet, and use other writers as models. Then, writers incorporate what they know with what they have learned as they revise and rewrite their writing.

Literature Connection

Bird by Bird: Some Instructions on Writing and Life by Anne Lamott

Teacher Tip

Good writers know how to find help to make their writing stronger. The following Student Activity Page guides students through the process of peer conferencing. As students work on their writing in pairs, you might want to provide additional support to students having difficulty thinking of specific, constructive comments.

Making the Connection

- Invite students to study the illustration on the card and discuss its message. (The young writer is having trouble—but fortunately, there are many sources of help available to her.)

- Explain that writers often need to seek out help when writing. They may need more information about their topic, or they may need help with the writing itself. Have students brainstorm ways of getting help for various writing challenges. Provide prompts such as: "Where could you find help in choosing the best word to convey a precise meaning? How can you get help focusing your ideas? Where can you turn if you need help writing a strong beginning?"

Connecting to Real Life

- Help students understand that even writers with many years of experience sometimes have to ask others for help. Read aloud the first sentence of Anne Lamott's "Acknowledgments" page from *Bird by Bird*: "I would like to acknowledge the extraordinary debt I owe to the writers who have told me such wise things about writing over the years. . . ." Together, brainstorm ways that writers might get help, directly and indirectly, from other writers.

- Explain that professional writers get help from editors, and often express thanks for this invaluable help in a book's acknowledgments section. Have students discuss how they can best duplicate an editor's help (listening to a trusted reader's advice, peer conferencing or peer editing, and so on).

- Point out that people are not the only source of help to writers. Together, discuss how reference books, the Internet, and other writers' models can provide assistance to writers.

Just for You

Form a partnership with another teacher/writer. Meet regularly to share samples of your writing, give and receive feedback and suggestions, talk over writing challenges, and inspire each other to make time for writing.

Writers get help.

Help! Writers request help often, and luckily, there are many sources of help available. Writers can find help from other people and from other writing. Then they use what they have learned to rewrite, revise, and improve their own work.

SOS: Help from Other People

Sometimes it's true that two heads are better than one. Try peer conferencing! Exchange writing drafts with a partner. Read your partner's work carefully. Then find a quiet corner to meet for a peer conference. Follow these guidelines:

- **Ask questions about anything you don't understand or that is confusing or unclear.**
- **Offer positive comments on parts of the writing you like (characters, dialogue, or descriptions).**
- **Offer specific suggestions for ways to improve the draft (a dramatic lead, more background material, stronger word choices, or varied sentence structure).**
- **No negative comments are allowed!**

SOS: Help from Other Writing

Sometimes you don't need help from a person; other writing can often provide just what you need to solve your writing problem.

Reread a draft of your writing. Then decide which of the following sources could provide ideas to help you improve your piece.

- reference books, such as a dictionary, thesaurus, or encyclopedia
- other nonfiction books
- a Web site
- other writers' books used as models or idea sources for style, beginnings, or dialogue

Now, think about what you have learned from other people and other writing. Rewrite your draft, using the help that you received.

Writers write for their readers.

In *Writing Rules!*, Mike Brusko says that students "generally start off with little or no idea what their reader looks like, let alone what his interests and needs are or what he expects to get from his reading. The result is usually writing that lacks clarity, focus, and purpose." The following activities help students think about their audience in order to write more effectively.

Making the Connection

- Have students examine the letters on the card. Ask students to compare Nick's letter to Tony with his letter to Grandpa. What is the same about the two letters? What is different? Why do they think Nick wrote two different letters?

- Point out that writers often tailor their writing for specific audiences, just as Nick did. Ask students to consider how a letter from Nick to his little brother might differ from his letters to Tony and Grandpa. What changes would he make when writing to a young child?

Connecting to Real Life

- Identify a class experience, such as a recent field trip. Have volunteers explain how a description of the trip written for the school principal might differ from one written to a close friend who missed the event. Ask students to describe how knowing the audience would affect the focus, language, and purpose of their letters. Then have half the class write about the trip for one audience and half write for the other audience. Pair students from both groups and have them share and compare their finished writing.

- Read aloud a passage from *Sideways Stories from Wayside School* or *Why Pick On Me (Marvin Redpost, 2)* by Louis Sachar. Ask students how they think an adult can know so much about young people's feelings and concerns. Explain that Sachar began to tune in to students' interests when he became a teacher's aide. He continues to spend time in schools and also to recall his experiences as a child in order to relate to his audience.

Just for You

Think about the next parent communication you will write. It may be a general notice to all of your students' families or a note to a particular parent. After you have written the piece, read your message while imagining that you are the intended audience. Does it come across the way you intended?

Literature Connection

Sideways Stories from Wayside School or *Why Pick on Me (Marvin Redpost, 2)* by Louis Sachar

Teacher Tip

On the following Student Activity Page students write for a specific audience and compare how knowing their audience affects their choice of words, use of imagery, rhyme pattern, and so on.

Writers write for their readers.

To be an effective writer, you must step into your readers' shoes. Thinking about the audience for your writing helps you choose your topic and affects the style and language of what you write. Try these activities to practice thinking about your audience.

Write a Handbook

Try writing for a specific audience—students who will be in fifth grade next year.

1. **Think about how fifth grade is similar to and different from fourth grade. Consider special things you have learned and done. Recall how you felt on your first day of fifth grade and what you would have liked to have known about fifth grade before you entered it.**
2. **Write a handbook for fourth graders that tells them what to expect next year. Offer some tips for success in fifth grade. You may want to include cartoon drawings or other illustrations.**
3. **Have a fourth grader read your draft. Ask if he or she has any suggestions for the handbook.**
4. **Present your revised handbook to a fourth grader or add it to your class book collection for new students to read when school starts next year.**

Write for a Different Audience

Write for two very different audiences.

1. **Choose a topic for a poem.**
2. **Think of two very different audiences, such as a kindergartner and the principal of your school. Consider how your writing would differ for each audience.**
3. **Write two poems on the same topic—one for each audience.**
4. **Compare and contrast your finished poems. Think about how knowing your audience affected your word choice, use of imagery, rhyme pattern, and so on.**
5. **If possible, present your writing to the appropriate audiences.**

Writers are reporters.

Teacher Tip

- On the following Student Activity Page students build their skills as journalists by writing one-paragraph articles using the 5W questions.
- Students also research events that happened in the past, and write historical reports.

Writers use all kinds of resources, such as research and interviews, to search for facts that they turn into reports or informational writing. Use these activities to help your students build their skills as reporters who learn about a topic and then share that information in writing.

Making the Connection

- Explain that the students pictured on the card are reading a school newspaper they have written. Initiate a discussion of how these reporters probably chose topics and gathered the information needed to write the articles. Ask students what articles they might include in a school newspaper and why.

- Point out that all students are reporters—whether or not they write for a newspaper. Help students realize that any time they write to share information they have learned, they are reporters. Have students recall topics they have addressed in report form. Discuss which they found to be interesting, and how they gathered information on those topics.

Connecting to Real Life

- Provide students with copies of a newspaper. Point out that newspaper reporters follow a set format when they write. In the first paragraph, they provide information to answer the 5W questions: *who, what, when, where,* and *why.* Subsequent paragraphs offer additional details about the topic. Have students work with partners to read an article and locate and identify the answers to the 5W questions.

- Have students create a list of report topics that interest them. Then ask a volunteer to choose a topic. Brainstorm questions a reader might have about the chosen topic, using the 5Ws as a guide. Then discuss ways a reporter might find answers to those questions. Stress to students that it is the reporter's responsibility to provide the background information readers need to understand the writing.

Just for You

Many people write seasonal letters to "report" to friends and relatives on happenings in their own lives and the lives of their immediate families. Make a web to show your recent activities and happenings and/or those of your family members. Consider writing a letter to report about the things listed on your web.

Name _____ Date _____

Writers are reporters.

Even if you don't work for a newspaper or magazine, you are still a reporter. When you research a topic and write about it to share what you have learned, you are writing to report. These activities help you build your reporting skills.

Answer Important Questions

As you know, a news reporter usually answers the questions *who, what, when, where,* and *why* in the first paragraph of an article. The remaining paragraphs provide more details about the topic. Try writing like a journalist.

1. **Choose an event related to your class, school, or community.**
2. **Write a one-paragraph article that includes answers to the 5W questions about the event.**
3. **Now brainstorm topic sentences for other paragraphs you could write about the event.**

Planning a Report on the Past

Newspaper reports usually concern events that are happening now, but reports can also be about things that happened in the past.

1. **Think about a time in history that interests you—ancient Egypt, pioneer days, or when your grandparents were your age, for example.**
2. **List some questions you have about that time period.**
3. **Brainstorm ideas about how you might find answers to your questions. Consider reference books, the Internet, interviews with people who lived during that time period, and so on.**
4. **Consider how you might present the information. For a historical report, you might want to present information in chronological order. Jot down a few notes about your organization ideas.**
5. **Now that your planning is done, research and write your report. Then share it with classmates.**

Writers send messages.

Teacher Tip

On the following Student
Activity Page students send
e-mails and write memos
to practice communicating
effectively.

Some of your students may well become poets, novelists, or journalists. *All* of your students, however, will use their writing skills to compose notes, letters, memos, and e-mails, now and in the future. These activities help students learn to communicate effectively.

Making the Connection

- Ask students to look at the card and describe what the girls are doing. (One has written an e-mail message, and the other has received it.) Have volunteers share their own experiences with e-mail.

- Ask students to identify other ways that they send messages to one another. For example, they write letters, memos, notes, lists, and postcards.

Connecting to Real Life

- Point out that adults send messages in their personal lives and at work. Share some messages you and other adults have written, such as memos, generic parent letters, phone message slips, postcards, and so on. Discuss how these messages are similar to and different from messages the students send.

- Ask students what characteristics they think good messages should have. Help them realize that, like any other form of writing, messages must communicate information clearly. Explain that when President Jimmy Carter took office, one of the first things he did was order all government workers to start writing clear, straightforward messages. Ask students why writing clear messages is important. (Misunderstood messages could have serious consequences; messages that are too long waste the reader's time; and so on.)

Just for You

Writing unexpected pleasant messages to friends, family members, students, or students' families can really help to brighten the recipient's day. Maybe you've been a lucky recipient and know this firsthand. Write or send an unexpected pleasant message to someone. He or she will appreciate it.

Writers send messages.

Think of the different kinds of messages you send at home and at school.
You will continue sending messages when you are an adult. Many of those
messages will be work-related—letters to customers, memos to the boss,
and e-mails to coworkers, for example. Learning to write clear messages
will help you now and in the future.

Send an E-mail

E-mail is a popular way to send messages. Think about people you can send e-mail
messages to. You probably have friends or family members who have access to e-mail.
Your teacher may be able to provide you with e-mail addresses for other fifth-grade
classes in your community or in others.

**Choose an e-mail recipient and plan your message. E-mail is less
formal than many other forms of communication. However, you
still need to be sure that your message is clear, logical, and free of
errors that can cause confusion.**

**Write your message. Then hit "Send." Check back later to see if you
got a response.**

Write a Memo

Memos are another common format for sending messages. A memo (short for
memorandum) is a quick way to communicate about a specific, focused matter.

**Write a memo to your teacher or a classmate. Tell about an
accomplishment, ask a question, give a reminder, make a complaint,
or offer an explanation. Be sure to use the following format at
the beginning of your memo:**

To: (the person you are writing to)

From: (your name)

Date: (today's date)

Regarding: (the subject of the memo)

Appendix:

Assessment Records, Checklists, and Conferencing

Ongoing Assessment Record

Assessment Technique or Tool	When to Record	Information Gathered	Form
Student Interview One-on-one with teacher Written responses Self-assessment	• First week of school • End of nine-week periods	• Interests • Attitudes toward reading and writing • Learning style • Instructional needs from teacher	pp. 174–175
Written Language Development Checklist Documentation of continuous observations	• Beginning of year • Periodically as information is observed from writing samples	• Matches observations to specific skills and strategies • Provides overview of strengths and needs	pp. 176–177
Writing Process Checklist Documentation of continuous observations	• Beginning of year • Periodically with writing projects and during writing workshop	• Matches observations to specific skills and behaviors • Shows use of writing process	p. 178
Writing Sample Self-assessment of own reading and writing	• End of first week • Middle of year • End of year	• Reading and writing interests, attitudes, and learning style	Creating Writing Rubrics, p. 179

Student Interview

Name: _____ **Grade :** _____ **Date:** _____

1. I like to read ❏ often ❏ sometimes ❏ not often ❏ never.

2. How important do you think reading and writing are to your life?_____

   _____

3. How important do you think reading and writing will be to your life in the future?

   _____

4. What do you like to do with your free time?_____

   _____

5. What is your favorite book of all time? Why is it your favorite? _____

   _____

6. What books have you read that you remember well enough to retell them to a friend?

   _____

   _____

7. Please check off the genres you like to read:

   ❏ newspapers   ❏ magazines   ❏ biography   ❏ poetry   ❏ science fiction

   ❏ humor   ❏ adventure   ❏ fantasy   ❏ historical fiction

   ❏ nonfiction (what kinds?)_____

   ❏ other _____

8. Please check off the types of writing you like to do:

   ❏ true stories   ❏ letters   ❏ poems   ❏ journal or diary

   ❏ reports   ❏ articles   ❏ songs   ❏ fiction stories

9. Do you have any favorite authors? List their names and what they wrote.

   _____

   _____

10. Please rate yourself as a reader:

    ❑ I need extra support when I read.

    ❑ I am an average reader who can read most things on my own.

    ❑ I am an above average reader because _____ .

11. What would you like to do better as a reader?

    ❑ understand what I read

    ❑ read hard books

    ❑ read faster

    ❑ other _____

12. What would you like to do better as a writer?

    ❑ choosing a topic

    ❑ organizing what I'm going to write

    ❑ writing a rough draft

    ❑ revising what I have written

    ❑ other _____

13. How do you prefer to read and work in the classroom?

    ❑ in a large group

    ❑ in small groups

    ❑ in pairs

14. Do you consider yourself better at reading or better at writing, or do you feel you do equally well at both?

    _____

15. My favorite school subject is _____ .

Written Language Development Checklist

Name: _____   Grade: _____

Date: _____   Age: _____

Selecting Topics – **Chooses to write a variety of fiction genres**	*Sometimes*	*Always*	*Never*
• Realistic			
• Historical Fiction			
• Humor			
• Adventure			
• Mystery			
• Fantasy			
• Fable			
• Science Fiction			
• Fairy Tales			
• Poetry			
• Other			
Selecting Topics – **Chooses to write a variety of nonfiction text types**			
• Narrative			
• True Events			
• Biography and Autobiography			
• Letters			
• Journals and Diaries			
• Informative			
• Interview			
• Historical Account			
• Description			
• Articles			
• Explanatory			
• Directions			
• Procedures			
• Fact/Opinion			
• Persuasive			
• Debate			
• Reference			
• Encyclopedia Entries			
• Dictionary			
• Atlas			
• Other			
• Selects writing genres and text types for specific purposes and audiences			
• Addresses topic, specific purpose, and audience when writing to prompts			

Written Language Development Checklist (continued)

Content and Message	Sometimes	Always	Never
• Narrows topic and maintains focus of the writing			
• Demonstrates knowledge of topic			
• Focuses on writing for a specific audience			
• Develops characters through thoughts, feelings, and actions			
• Uses appropriate dialogue in a purposeful way			
• Develops an engaging plot			
• Defines setting			
• Makes transitions in time, setting, and point of view			
• Presents information in a logical sequence			
Structure and Development of Ideas			
• Develops effective leads			
• Uses a variety of endings			
• Varies sentence structures			
• Builds paragraphs			
• Organizes paragraphs effectively			
• Develops beginning, middle, and ending			
• Presents main ideas and supporting details			
• Uses nonfiction text type structures			
• Compare/contrast			
• Cause/effect			
• Problem/solution			
Craft			
• Uses multiple adjectives and adverbs to describe			
• Uses figures of speech			
• Describes actions and events to "show" rather than "tell"			
• Experiments with new vocabulary			
• Creates a "voice" in writing pieces			
• Selective in word choice to convey meaning			
• Adds depth in description with the five senses			
Writing Conventions: Grammar, Punctuation, Capitalization, Spelling			
• Uses complete sentences with correct word order			
• Demonstrates understanding of subject–verb agreement			
• Writes simple and complex grammatically correct sentences			
• Uses singular and plural nouns correctly			
• Uses basic capitalization rules			
• Uses basic punctuation rules			
• Makes many close spelling approximations			
• Writes more correct spellings than approximations			

Writing Process Checklist

Name: _____ Grade: _____

Date: _____ Age: _____

	Sometimes	Always	Never
Prewriting			
• Manages writing, organizes ideas, uses writing strategies			
• Notes and lists writing ideas and topics			
• Organizes ideas for writing fiction (graphic organizers)			
• Organizes ideas for writing nonfiction			
• Uses and refers to books as writing models for fiction and nonfiction			
Drafting			
• Uses rough draft as a working document for revision			
• Works independently to develop ideas			
• Questions and asks for response when needed			
• Manages time to work toward completion			
Revising			
• Uses reference tools for revision and editing			
• Adds description and details			
• Considers word choice			
• Deletes unnecessary information			
• Revises to improve flow and clarity of ideas			
• Moves text when needed			
• Uses proofreading symbols			
• Checks grammar and usage			
• Checks capitalization			
• Checks punctuation			
• Checks spelling			
• Rereads work and seeks a reading from peers and teacher for feedback on editing and revising			
• Conferences with peers and teacher for revision ideas and feedback			
Publishing			
• Brings select writing pieces to completion			
• Refers to criteria for publishing			
• Selects authentic purposes and audiences to submit writing			
Assessment			
• Uses self-assessment techniques and tools (rubrics, checklists)			
• Conferences with peers and teacher			
• Analyzes writing and responds with writing log			

© 2002 Rigby

178   *Wonder Writers*

Creating Writing Rubrics

Rubrics are assessment tools, which include descriptions of writing characteristics with skills and strategies and scoring guides for student writing samples.

Suggestions for Designing and Using a Rubric

1. Determine the characteristics of writing that students need in order to compose quality writing pieces.
2. Determine specific skills and strategies to teach and assess.
3. Determine the criteria for scoring the writing characteristics of the student's piece.
4. Use models of rubrics to match your writing process instruction—
   - Use published rubrics.
   - Revise rubrics to be more personalized for your classroom.
   - Create your own rubrics specific to what you are teaching.
   - Create rubrics with students for involvement in self-assessment.
   - Refer to state standards.

Example of a Rubric for a Fiction Writing Piece

Message and Content	Score
(Specific skills and strategies)	
• Creates an engaging plot	
• Defines setting	
• Uses details	
Structure and Organization	
• Makes transitions in time, setting, and point of view	
• Develops beginning, middle, end	
Craft	
• Creates voice	
• Shows rich word choice	
Conventions	
• Uses correct spelling	
• Uses correct punctuation	

Criteria for Scoring

1 = Not evident
2 = Beginning use, but more need for revisions than strength
3 = Strengths and need for revisions about equal
4 = Evident use with some revision needed
5 = Very strong and purposefully used

Student Writing Portfolios

Student writing portfolios help students:
- collect meaningful writing pieces
- organize their writing
- self-assess to reflect on their strengths and needs
- see their progress over time
- set writing goals
- revisit their writing pieces to develop ideas
- have ownership and responsibility for their writing
- provide examples and discussion points for student/teacher conferences

Writing Samples

The writing samples are selected by the students to showcase themselves as writers! Students select their writing samples and explain why they selected the pieces to be part of their portfolio to assess their writing. On forms or sticky notes attached to the writing they may answer the following:
- Why did I select this piece?
- What does it show about me as a writer?

Encourage students to include an array of samples to show different types of writing for different purposes, such as:
- Samples of fiction that show understanding of the features of genres
- Responses to literature that show understanding of literary elements
- Samples of nonfiction that show the understanding structures and features of nonfiction text types
- Samples of writing across the curriculum that show reading and writing connections
- Literature responses that show creativity through art, music, writing, drama
- Writing that shows the student's use of the reading process by including the first draft, revised drafts, and all writing to the final published copy

Writing Records and Assessments
- List of writing ideas
- Record of completed writing pieces
- Record of pieces drafted
- Self-assessments
- Writing goals
- Genre lists

Teacher Tips for Writing Conferences

As writers draft, they need to talk about their writing and get responses to their writing from their peers and teacher as they make decisions during the revision process. By conferring with students, you can respond to the student and the student's writing as you also model the art of conferring. Students leave the conference with ideas for revision, and the experience helps them learn to conference independently with their peers.

Move and Manage Time

- Go to the students to conference with them
- Take paper, sticky notes, and a pencil with you
- Facilitate short, focused conferences

Listen Carefully

- Let the writer read his or her writing or parts of the writing
- Give one-on-one attention

Personalize the Responses

- Be specific in praise
- Keep a low voice
- Use sensory responses
- Acknowledge growth
- Identify strategies, skills and techniques
- Tell what you "heard"
- Reread/paraphrase words or lines
- Offer ideas and solutions as requested

Ask Helpful, Focused Questions

- How is your writing coming along?
- How can I help you?
- Where did this (word, idea, sentence) come from?
- How did you solve this?
- Where are you going with the piece?
- What do you plan to do next?

Finding/Recording Ideas for a Writer's Notebook

September 20th

We went to the state fair today and saw a quilt exhibit. I thought it would be boring, but it wasn't! There were all kinds of quilts—old and new. The designs were awesome. A few quilts had pictures created in cloth. Others were made of squares, triangles, and other shapes. And some were absolutely WILD—with different colors and patterns all scrambled up in one design. I heard someone say that one quilt has tens of thousands of tiny, tiny stitches in it. Can you imagine how long it takes to make one???

September 22nd

Dad and I went to the pond after dinner today. The water was like a mirror! I leaned over to look at myself and ended up getting my feet wet. I saw a whole flock of geese floating around in the middle of the pond. They'll be heading south pretty soon, I guess. I love to listen to them honking and squawking. Just before we left, the whole flock took off at once—as if someone had given a signal. You could hear the sound of their wings flapping. It was cool!

Gorgeous feathered birds
Eating water plants
Eating bugs
So lovely as they float
Even lovelier when they soar.

An acrostic poem!

Three Excerpts

Oh, didn't I feel sorry for myself when the Wabash Railroad's Blue Bird train steamed into Grandma's town. The sandwich was still crumbs in my throat because I didn't have the dime for a bottle of pop.
(Richard Peck, <u>A Year Down Yonder</u>, Chapter 1)

He pulled at his snout and chewed his lips. He was beginning to comprehend the awkwardness of his position. He was marooned on an island, nowhere near civilization, as far as he could tell; and if he was going to get off, it must be by his own devices.
(William Steig, <u>Abel's Island</u>, Chapter 4)

As Ramona sat on the hard edge of the tub, feeling sorry for herself and trying to sort out her thoughts, she noticed a brand-new red-white-and-blue tube of toothpaste lying beside the washbasin. . . . I'll give it one little squeeze, thought Ramona. Just one teeny tiny squeeze to make me feel better . . . She squeezed again. Another satisfying squirt. She felt even better.
(Beverly Cleary, <u>Ramona and Her Mother</u>, Chapter 2)

Writing Paragraphs (without indents)

Kim was looking forward to her eleventh birthday for many reasons. She was hoping Grandpa would surprise her with a new tennis racket. Mom would bake one of her yummy chocolate cakes; Kim could taste it already! But the best and most important thing about turning eleven was that eleven-year-olds could volunteer at Hartland Hospital. Kim, who'd wanted to be a doctor since she was eight, could hardly wait. At Hartland Hospital, Sara Doyle practiced her speech to welcome new volunteers. She was in charge of training volunteers, and she loved meeting the youngsters and seeing their enthusiasm. "What are you doing, Sara?" asked Dr. Tyler. "I'm planning for our new volunteers. I wonder if any of them will become a nurse or doctor someday."

Writing Paragraphs (with indents)

Kim was looking forward to her eleventh birthday for many reasons. She was hoping Grandpa would surprise her with a new tennis racket. Mom would bake one of her yummy chocolate cakes; Kim could taste it already! But the best and most important thing about turning eleven was that eleven-year-olds could volunteer at Hartland Hospital. Kim, who'd wanted to be a doctor since she was eight, could hardly wait.

At Hartland Hospital, Sara Doyle practiced her speech to welcome new volunteers. She was in charge of training volunteers, and she loved meeting the youngsters and seeing their enthusiasm.

"What are you doing, Sara?" asked Dr. Tyler.

"I'm planning for our new volunteers. I wonder if any of them will become a nurse or doctor someday."

Writing with Clarity

Passage 1

I look up at the sky. Somewhere amid all of those stars was the Big Dipper, the most well-known of all. I knew it was shaped like a large spoon. Or ladle. I looked for pointer stars at the end. Spotting it is easy. I imagine a line connected these stars and extending upward. I knew this always pointed north to the North Star. I locate the North Star, and I knew it.

Passage 2

I look up at the sky. Somewhere amid all of those stars is the Big Dipper, the most well-known of all the constellations. It is shaped like a large spoon or ladle, and its shape is easy to spot.

Next I look for the two stars, called "pointer stars," that form the end of the spoon's bowl. I imagine a line connecting these two stars and extending upward. I know that this imaginary line always points to the North Star. When I locate the North Star, I know which way is north.

Point of View Chart

	_____'s Point of View Story Title: _____ _____	_____'s Point of View Story Title: _____ _____
Character or Event		
Character or Event		
Character or Event		
Character or Event		

Five-Paragraph Essay Format

1. Introductory Paragraph 1
    - topic sentence _____
    - three subtopics that support the topic sentence _____
    _____
    _____
    _____

2. Body Paragraph 2
    - topic sentence (first subtopic) _____
    - three supporting details _____
    _____
    _____

3. Body Paragraph 3
    - topic sentence (second subtopic) _____
    - three supporting details _____
    _____
    _____

4. Body Paragraph 4
    - topic sentence (third subtopic) _____
    - three supporting details _____
    _____
    _____

5. Concluding Paragraph 5
    - restates the topic _____
    _____
    _____

© 2002 Rigby

The Case for Sneakers

There is no doubt that sneakers are the most sensible shoes ever created. First, they are the most comfortable shoes. They are perfect for active sports as well as day-to-day walking. Feet never get tired or sore in sneakers.

Sneakers also look great. Everyone can find a style that pleases them. When you have sneakers, you don't have to worry about what to put on your feet every morning. A good pair of sneakers goes with everything. Being a sneaker enthusiast makes dressing your feet easy and fun.

Wearing sneakers sends a message to other people. It says that the wearer keeps up with the latest trends. It also communicates that the person is casual and fun. Shiny leather shoes could never give that message.

Some people complain that the cost of sneakers continues to go up and up. When you consider that you can't buy a better style of shoe, the price is worth it.

America's Favorite Shoe

Sneakers are the best-loved shoes in America today. These shoes are all-occasion footwear. People use them for school, work, and play. Americans buy more than 150 million pairs of sneakers a year. As a result, almost nine out of ten people have at least one pair of sneakers in their closets.

Sneakers may be so popular because there is an enormous variety of choices. A look at the racks in a shoe or sporting goods store will prove that sneakers come in every color and style you can imagine.

People also like wearing sneakers because they associate them with professional athletes. Many people admire athletes and want to imitate them. This is why sneaker ads often feature stars like Michael Jordan. Ron Duquette of Oregon is a good example of someone who has fallen in love with sneakers. He collects shoes that were once owned by professional athletes. He has more than 170 pairs in his collection.

Another reason that sneakers are America's best-loved shoes is that people are willing to spend more and more money to cover their feet in the latest sneaker style. Americans spend over two billion dollars each year on kids' sneakers alone.

No other shoe in American history has been loved as much and as long as sneakers. Considering that designers introduce new styles every six months, the American love affair with the sneaker is likely to continue.

Business Letter

423 High Street
Smallville, IN 31115
March 22, 2002

Terry Evans, President
Wonder Toy Company
1 Ross Road
New York, NY 10000

Dear Mr. Evans:

   I am returning the Science Wonder Puzzle I bought from your company. I got the puzzle for my little brother for his fifth birthday. The box said it was for children from four through seven. Neither my brother nor any of his friends could do the puzzle. It was way too hard for them.

   Please refund my money. If you have any questions, you can call me at 555-555-1111. Thank you for your help.

Sincerely,
Pat Warner

Memo

Sunny Springs Public Library
111 Mayfield Way
Baltimore, Maryland 20000

Let us help you find everything you need!

Date: September 4, 2002

To: Fifth Grade Students

From: Jerry Martin, Children's Librarian

Re: Homework Helper Program

The Sunny Springs Public Library is excited to announce a new program for fifth grade students. Starting October 1, you can sign up for 30-minute sessions with one of our library volunteers, who will help you find the best books, magazines, and Internet sources for your school projects. We will show you where to look for materials that are useful for science projects, social studies reports, and writing assignments. We will not do the job for you, but we will make it a lot easier for you to find what you need.

To learn more about this new service, come to the orientation session from 9 to 10 A.M. on September 18. If you have questions, ask your parents to call 410-555-5555.

News Article

Mt. Washington Neighborhood News

Treat Your Family to a Day of Fun!

If the kids are getting cranky because they are running out of things to do this summer, put them in the car on August 3 and head for the Mt. Washington Summer Fair. This year, as in the past, there will be a variety of activities for toddlers through teens. Moms, dads, and grandparents can spend the entire day cheering their children on in races and contests. Mt. Washington parents are preparing plenty of healthful treats for sale. A big hit of the day is always the children's used book sale, where parents can buy gently used children's books for very low prices. Admission to the fair is still only $5.00 for adults and $1.00 for children.

News Article

Mt. Washington Elementary School Newsletter

Mt. Washington Summer Fair

Why is the first Saturday in August one of the most fun days of the summer? It's the day that Mt. Washington Elementary School holds its annual summer fair. This year the fair will be on August 3 from 10 A.M. until 5 P.M. Many activities are planned for children of all ages. There will be relay races, eating contests, and exciting rides. At noon, a mystery guest will perform in the school auditorium. When fair goers get thirsty and hungry from all the activities, they can buy frosty lemonades, tasty sandwiches, and fruit ices. The Mt. Washington Fair is always a great place to see school and neighborhood friends, have fun, and talk about summer vacations.

Deleting Unnecessary Information

"Mom, I don't want to go camping across the country this summer," Lee whined, stomping up the stairs that were covered with green carpet.

"You'll have fun," his mother yelled to him. "Jenny, please set the table for dinner."

Lee responded, "But Mom, I won't see my friends all summer."

Lee ran into his room and closed the door. He noticed his book on the desk. He was dreading summer.

Self-Assessment Chart

Title:
Genre:

I am proud of . . .	I want to improve . . .	A technique to try is . . .

Writing Log Assessment Chart

Name _____   Writing Log for _____

My Strengths	Writing Examples

Goals for Next Month

Rigby Literacy Comprehension Quarterly Teaching Sequence

Issue Number	Comprehension Quarterly	Mini-Lesson	Strategy Card
5.1	All That Glitters	41, 46, 51, 88	1, 2
5.2	Nighttime Notebook	42, 47, 54, 89	3, 4
5.3	Don't Make Me Laugh!	43, 55, 77, 100	5, 6
5.4	Eye Openers	44, 49, 52, 66	7, 8
5.5	Gobs of Goo	50, 53, 57, 104	9, 10
5.6	From Comics to Classics	48, 59, 68, 103	11, 12
5.7	Scavenger Hunt	45, 60, 67, 87	13, 14
5.8	Dare to Dream	62, 70, 74, 75	15, 16
5.9	Weird and Wonderful	61, 71, 81, 91	17, 18
5.10	Short Stuff	58, 80, 82, 93	19, 20
5.11	Fooled Again	65, 78, 90, 95	21, 22
5.12	The Main Character	63, 73, 85, 94	23, 24
5.13	Castles, Cabins, and Capsules	64, 79, 92, 96	25, 26
5.14	Go Away!	56, 69, 76, 97	27, 28
5.15	Keep Your Balance	72, 86, 98, 101	29, 30
5.16	Life in a Crowded Place	83, 84, 99, 102	31, 32

Professional Resources

After the End: Teaching and Learning Creative Revision by Barry Lane, Heinemann, 1993. The author focuses on revision throughout the writing process to promote quality writing.

Conversations: Strategies for Teaching, Learning, and Evaluating by Regie Routman, Heinemann, 2000. Regie Routman continues her literacy conversation and offers practical, field-tested ideas and strategies for teaching writing.

Craft Lessons: Teaching Writing K–8 by Ralph Fletcher and Joann Portalupi, Stenhouse Publishers, 1998. The authors present organized writing lessons to support teachers as they work with children who craft their own writing pieces.

A Fresh Look at Writing by Donald Graves, Heinemann, 1994. Donald Graves presents the latest ideas on teaching writing in a comprehensive resource for new teachers as well as master teachers.

Lasting Impressions: Weaving Literature into the Writing Workshop by Shelley Harwayne, Heinemann, 1992. Shelley Harwayne, a New York City principal, shares stories of real children and her own love of literature as she reexamines the structure and dynamics of the writing workshop.

Living Between the Lines by Lucy Calkins, Heinemann, 1990. Lucy Calkins' presentation of the reading-writing workshop details the use of writers' notebooks to establish real-life reading and writing connections.

Nonfiction Craft Lessons: Teaching Information Writing K–8 by Joann Portalupi and Ralph Fletcher, Stenhouse, 2001. The authors present detailed writing lessons to support students as they learn to write informational pieces.

Nonfiction Matters: Reading, Writing, and Research in Grades 3–8 by Stephanie Harvey, Stenhouse Publishers, 1998. The teacher researcher presents strategies and ideas for teaching nonfiction writing.

What a Writer Needs by Ralph Fletcher, Heinemann, 1993. Ralph Fletcher focuses on helping children improve as writers by providing specific practical strategies for challenging and extending students' writing.

Writing: Teachers and Children at Work by Donald Graves, Heinemann, 1983. This Donald Graves classic describes the learning theory and classroom practice of the writing workshop.

Notes